CHRISTIANS&JEWS
IN DIALOGUE

CHRISTIANS&JEWS IN DIALOGUE

LEARNING IN THE PRESENCE OF THE OTHER

MARY C. BOYS
SARA S. LEE

FOREWORD BY DOROTHY C. BASS

Walking Together, Finding the Way ®
SKYLIGHT PATHS®
PUBLISHING
Woodstock, Vermont

Christians and Jews in Dialogue:
Learning in the Presence of the Other

2006 First Printing
© 2006 by Mary C. Boys and Sara S. Lee

Grateful acknowledgment is given for permission to use excerpts from *Faith Transformed: Christian Encounters with Jews and Judaism* by John C. Merkle, ed., copyright 2003. Used by permission of Liturgical Press.

Library of Congress Cataloging-in-Publication Data
Boys, Mary C.
Christians and Jews in dialogue : learning in the presence of the other / by Mary C. Boys and Sara S. Lee.
    p. cm.
Includes bibliographical references.
ISBN-13: 978-1-59473-144-0
ISBN-10: 1-59473-144-6
1. Christianity and other religions—Judaism. 2. Judaism—Relations—Christianity. 3. Boys, Mary C. 4. Lee, Sara S., 1933– 5. Christianity and other religions—Judaism—Study and teaching. 6. Judaism—Relations—Christianity—Study and teaching. 7. Dialogue—Religious aspects—Christianity. 8. Dialogue—Religious aspects—Judaism. 9. Religious pluralism—United States. I. Lee, Sara S., 1933– II. Title.

BM535.B649 2006
261.2'6—dc22
                                                        2006018547
10 9 8 7 6 5 4 3 2 1
Manufactured in the United States of America
Jacket design: Sara Dismukes

> SkyLight Paths Publishing is creating a place where people of different spiritual traditions come together for challenge and inspiration, a place where we can help each other understand the mystery that lies at the heart of our existence.
>
> SkyLight Paths sees both believers and seekers as a community that increasingly transcends traditional boundaries of religion and denomination—people wanting to learn from each other, walking together, finding the way.

SkyLight Paths, "Walking Together, Finding the Way" and colophon are trademarks of LongHill Partners, Inc., registered in the U.S. Patent and Trademark Office.

Walking Together, Finding the Way®
Published by SkyLight Paths Publishing
A Division of LongHill Partners, Inc.
Sunset Farm Offices, Route 4, P.O. Box 237
Woodstock, VT 05091
Tel: (802) 457-4000   Fax: (802) 457-4004
www.skylightpaths.com

To those Jews and Christians who,
in studying in the presence of the other,
have also enriched us.

CONTENTS

FOREWORD

The United States is today a country where many religious traditions flourish. Yet we, the people, have yet to determine how we shall come to terms with this exciting but potentially troubling reality. The question of how to be religious people in a pluralistic context is not only a constitutional and political one, after all. Our responses to this question also shape our sense of who we are as individuals, families, and communities.

In a pluralistic context where particularist religious commitments sometimes reflect past grievances or erupt in present-day conflict, it is not surprising that some people respond by toning down their religious identity and seeking refuge in relatively bland and private spiritualities. On the other hand, those who have experienced God's presence in the practices of an enduring tradition find that response deeply unsatisfying. These more observant and believing ones sense how impoverished they, and humanity as a whole, would be without the rich and complex wisdom these traditions bear. And so, hoping to sustain them, some retreat into enclaves of the like-minded.

Often they show tolerance toward those of different faith, but they never really get to know them or to appreciate their approach to the sacred. This ignorance can even keep them from recognizing some of the rich and distinctive gifts they receive from their own tradition.

Christians and Jews in Dialogue: Learning in the Presence of the Other offers a third alternative. In this important book, a knowledgeable and committed Jew and a knowledgeable and committed Catholic demonstrate that it is possible to approach one another's tradition with understanding and respect. Indeed, they show that in doing so one may find one's own particularity both expanded and enriched. Beyond this, moreover, they argue that the mature and ethical embrace of each tradition requires such mutual understanding and respect. These do not result simply from good will but rather from serious study undertaken in the context of honest and persistent interpersonal relationships.

Sara Lee and Mary Boys demonstrate here the transformative potential of excellent religious education. In an age when many educated people fear that religious difference will be the undoing of the world, these authors argue that religious education holds the key to reconciliation among those of different religious traditions. And at a time when many religious leaders seek to build fortresses of communal identity as defenses against religious pluralism, these authors see religious education as the surest path to a just, secure, and even joyful pluralism.

The "textured particularism" advocated by these two compassionate and committed women is, appropriately, particular to them and to their traditions. This book and the other work Sara and Mary have done together focus intently on Judaism and Catholicism and the painful history of the relationship between these two traditions. Early in the book, both women share moving religious autobiographies that offer powerful insights into the impact of early misconceptions of the other and the healing effects of growing knowledge of the other later in life. I deeply admire the commitment of both women to persevere in the path of interreligious learning in spite of the legacy of oppression and suspicion carried by Jewish heirs of their shared history and the legacy of shame inherited by Catholics. Their compassionate persistence even in the face of pain—their own and that of their students—has enabled them to invite many colearners into a more truthful understanding of the other and a more mature appropriation of their own religious legacy.

The dialogue between this Catholic and this Jew, then, is a particular one involving two traditions that have a specific, complex, and formative relationship with one another. Thus the book does not and cannot address how interreligious learning might serve the many other alienated traditions and communities that exist all over the world. This refusal to generalize is appropriate to Mary and Sara's emphasis on the interpersonal and tradition-specific demands of interreligious learning. However, their account does make me long to see religious educators from other families of faith explore the potential of this approach. It also makes me long to see dialogue that takes seriously and addresses the deep antagonisms that exist within each tradition, including the Protestant Christianity where I make my religious home. But that is a task for another day and other educators.

I have had the privilege of participating in Sara and Mary's work at several points along the way. In 1995, I attended a session of the Catholic-Jewish Colloquium, which gathered an impressive and committed group of Jewish and Catholic educators for sustained "learning in the presence of the other," as this book's subtitle puts it. What I saw there was educational teamwork of the highest order. The qualities that make Mary Boys and Sara Lee exceptionally gifted teachers were evident at every turn: both are deeply grounded in and knowledgeable of their own traditions, passionate about the well-being of the other's religious community, and personally strong enough to

listen with patience and discernment. Calling attention to their
gifts, however, may deflect attention from the painstaking
work they put into each educational encounter. The guidance
on teaching they offer in chapter 5, which includes a summary
of the kinds of questions they asked as they prepared for each
colloquium meeting or other class or workshop, not only
reports on their own practice but also provides immensely
helpful advice for other educators. Those inspired by Sara and
Mary's example to attempt interreligious teaching and learning
in their own context must take this seriously: to do this, you
must commit yourself to very careful planning and preparation. Those who teach other subjects of deep personal and
social importance should also heed this advice.

My second opportunity to participate in interreligious learning with Mary and Sara, as they report in chapter 7, came during
our 1997 trip to Israel. Memories of the places we visited and the
conversations we shared continue to shape how I hear certain
biblical narratives and how I understand the historical significance of the Shoah. These memories also deepen the sorrow I feel
each time I hear of violence in Jerusalem. I am immensely grateful to these two wise and generous women for welcoming me into
their journey on that occasion and across the years.

Now this book also welcomes you, dear readers, into their
remarkable journey. I commend it to you with confidence that
the stories, methods, and challenges it conveys will deepen
your understanding of what is at stake in efforts to address the
hostility and ignorance that have too often divided Christians
and Jews. More important, I commend it to you with hope that
it will strengthen your commitment and enlarge your capacity
to contribute to the healing of the world.

Dorothy C. Bass
Valparaiso, Indiana

ACKNOWLEDGMENTS

The process of writing brought to mind the many wonderful persons who have participated in our projects, and it is to them we dedicate this book.

We acknowledge grants from the Lilly Endowment and the Valparaiso Project on the Education and Formation of People in Faith that funded several of our projects. We are grateful also for support from the Center for Christian-Jewish Learning at Boston College, and for Mary's sabbatical leave as a Henry Luce III Fellow in Theology, granted by the Henry Luce Foundation, Inc., and the Association of Theological Schools.

We thank colleagues who provided helpful comments on various chapters: Eva Fleischner; Jill Morehouse Lum; Michael McGarry, C.S.P.; Stephanie Ruskay; Michelle Lynn-Sachs; Lesley A. Sacouman, S.N.J.M.; and Kathleen Talvacchia. We also thank Beth Nichols for interviewing selected participants in our various projects and Rachel A. Bundang for helping to ready the manuscript for the publisher. We are indebted to the generosity of Dorothy Bass in writing the foreword.

The professional editing skills of Barbara King Lord were invaluable in blending and refining our voices. Her care and expertise have contributed immeasurably to this book, and we are most grateful.

Finally, we thank our families, friends, and colleagues for their support.

INTRODUCTION

This is the story of two educators, one a Jew (Sara Lee) and the other a Catholic nun (Mary Boys), who for twenty years have designed and led projects in "interreligious learning" as a means of reconciliation between their traditions. This is a story of friendship that enabled candid conversations across boundaries of religious difference and sustained mutual trust even when confronting painful issues. And this is the story of the power of education in healing religious division.

The story begins with our conviction that religions must become a catalyst in reducing the world's conflicts. We focus especially on our own Jewish and Catholic Christian traditions in which the tragic relationship of the past now enjoys the possibility of a new bond. Then in chapters 2 and 3, we tell something of our own stories, sharing a bit of what has formed us and the personal impact of our involvements in Christian-Jewish dialogue. In chapter 4 we describe our shared projects, and in chapter 5 we analyze the educational thinking that shaped those projects. Chapter 6 looks at the Holocaust through the lens of our trip to Auschwitz in 2004, and chapter 7 examines the complexities of the Land of Israel in light of our journey there in 1997. We offer a brief concluding word in chapter 8 through the testimony of some who took part in our projects.

A word on how we have coordinated the two voices of this book: In some chapters, one of us has done the initial draft, and then we have reviewed it together to produce the final version. Those chapters are written in the first person plural. In other chapters, however, our voices alternate, using first person singular. We have also reviewed these chapters together. Each of our biographical chapters is written exclusively in our own voice.

Christians and Jews in Dialogue: Learning in the Presence of the Other flows out of years of conversation. We hope that in entering into our conversation, readers will learn not only about the potential of interreligious learning but also the hope it engenders.

1

JEWS AND CHRISTIANS: A COMPLICATED RELATIONSHIP

> There can be no peace among the nations without peace among the religions. There can be no peace among the religions without dialogue between the religions. There can be no dialogue between the religions without research into theological foundations.[1]

A neighborhood stroll, especially in large urban areas such as Los Angeles and New York City, can be an eye-opening experience, given the myriad houses of worship. Traditional and nontraditional, these sacred places lining the streets testify that more religions are practiced in the United States than in any other country in the world.[2] More important, they represent the richness of religious diversity, always one of the world's treasures, and now, thanks to mass global communication, one that is more and more widely realized.

But recognition of difference constitutes neither understanding nor acceptance. In far too many cases, religious difference fuels conflict. Violence in the name of religion continues to scar many parts of the world, whether between Hindus and Muslims in India, Orthodox Serbs and Muslims in the Balkans, or Protestants and Catholics in Northern Ireland. In 2005–2006, twelve cartoons portraying the prophet Muhammad appearing in a small Danish paper, *Jyllands-Posten*, ignited a massive controversy that led to violent protests from Nigeria to the Middle East. In France and Belgium, right-wing Christian groups associated with the "Identity Bloc" have organized soup kitchens that serve only soups made with pork products—thereby excluding Muslims and Jews. One of the leaders of a Paris soup-kitchen group says, "Our freedom in France is being threatened. If we prefer European civilization and Christian culture, that's our choice."[3]

Religion alone is not the cause of such violence, but, as Rabbi Jonathan Sacks says, it "forms the fault-line along which sides divide," thereby intensifying conflict rather than lessening it.[4] Religion is but a component—albeit a significant one—of the struggles we humans have in living respectfully with difference. When combined with factors such as rage, racism, xenophobia, or nationalism, religion is dangerous.

Rabbi Sacks asks in an earlier work whether religions are ready for the "greatest challenge they have ever faced, namely a world in which even local conflict can have global repercussions." In his view, the fate of the twenty-first century may turn on whether the world's religions can "make a space for those who are not its adherents, who sing a different song, hear a different music, tell a different story."[5]

Yet negative judgments about the religious other, however dangerous in our time, are not entirely surprising. Tolerance of religious diversity threatens what many of us were taught to believe. Often religious teaching itself provides a barrier to tolerance. Although we could give many examples, we will restrict ourselves to a word about our own traditions.

MAKING SPACE FOR RELIGIOUS DIFFERENCE:
A CHALLENGE TO CHRISTIANITY AND JUDAISM

Although today the Catholic Church expresses considerable regard for other religions, such respect contrasts with earlier attitudes. The documents from the Second Vatican Council (1962–65) differ dramatically from earlier councils, such as the Council of Florence, which, in its 1442 "Decree for the Copts," claimed that "no one remaining outside the Catholic Church, not only pagans, but also Jews, heretics or schismatics, can become partakers of eternal life; but they will go to the 'eternal fire prepared for the devil and his angels' [Matt. 25:41], unless before the end of their life they are received into it." This decree ends with the chilling statement, "And no one can be saved, no matter how much alms he has given, even if he sheds his blood for the name of Christ, unless he remains in the bosom and unity of the Catholic Church."[6] There was no space for those who were not church members.

In contrast, Vatican II refers to Jews as a people who remain "most dear to God," and Muslims as those who also adore the "one and merciful God." It speaks of those "who through no fault of their own do not know the Gospel of Christ or His Church, yet sincerely seek God and moved by grace strive by their deeds to do His will as it is known to them through the dictates of conscience." They also "can attain to salvation"—a clear counterpoint to the Council of Florence.

This reversal of attitude in official Catholic teaching about other religions is still developing and debated. By no means have all the complex questions concerning the relationship of Catholic Christianity to other religions been resolved. No theological consensus exists with regard to adjudicating the truth claims of other religious traditions. Similarly, many of the so-called mainline Protestant churches reveal a new openness to the religious other without having solved the theological questions. The rich and abundant literature addressing these questions testifies to their depth and breadth.[7]

In other Christian circles, however, belief systems have little room for the religious other. For example, students, officers, faculty, and trustees at Patrick Henry College, a nondenominational Christian college in Purcellville, Virginia, must sign a ten-part "Statement of Faith" that includes the claims that salvation "is exclusively found by faith alone in Jesus Christ and His shed blood" and that hell is the place "where all who die outside of Christ shall be confined in conscious torment for eternity."[8] Such beliefs, in effect, reduce the world's diverse religions to two categories: followers of Jesus Christ, who alone can be saved from the torment of hell, and nonbelievers, who have no hope of salvation.

Jewish views regarding other religions are similarly diverse, and equally difficult to summarize in a systematic fashion. Jewish textual sources contain contrasting and sometimes contradictory views. One point on which sources seem to agree is the belief that only Jews are obligated to observe Jewish law. Non-Jews are subject to the seven so-called "Noahide commandments": prohibitions against murder, idolatry, incest, eating a limb torn from a living animal, blasphemy, theft, and the requirement to establish laws and courts.[9] Observing these more universal commandments was viewed as what God required of non-Jews and deemed sufficient to warrant God's blessing: "The pious and virtuous of all nations can participate in eternal bliss."[10] Yet this does not answer the question of how Jews are to regard other religious systems.

Traditionally, idolatry has been the primary category through which other religions are evaluated. In the Jewish view, idolatry is the most serious breach in any relationship to God. Born out of the Israelites' experience with idol worshippers, and the necessity of making a clear distinction between such worship and monotheism, both biblical and rabbinic sources reject idolatry with vehemence. In fact, the tractate *Avodah Zarah* in the Mishnah and Talmud is devoted to the subject of idolatry.[11] They give considerable attention to laws governing the relationships between Jews and potential idol worshippers, forbidding, for example, contact with them or sharing of property. Jewish texts regard idolatry as more than an immoral practice that Judaism rejected. Worshipping any part of God's creation was seen as "making part of reality the whole of it, taking one of God's creatures as God himself."[12] Thus, a number of medieval Jewish commentators held that Islam was not idolatrous, but that Christianity might be because of Christian doctrines of the Trinity and the claim that Jesus was divine. The overwhelming bias of Jewish jurisprudence in the past supports the judgment that Christian practices are at least potentially idolatrous.

Even the changes initiated by the Second Vatican Council did not change the view of some contemporary Jewish legal authorities in the most traditional wings of Orthodoxy. In 1967, a young Orthodox rabbi asked Rabbi Moshe Feinstein, recognized throughout the Jewish world for his scholarship as an interpreter and a *posek* (Hebrew for a "decisor," one who is authorized to render legal decisions in response to questions of Jewish law), about participation in a Christian-Jewish dialogue. Rabbi Feinstein ruled that such participation would be "a grave violation of the prohibition against appurtenances to idolatry."[13] Rabbi Feinstein clearly stood with those medieval commentators who viewed Christianity as potentially idolatrous. He tried to generate support from another great scholar, Rabbi Joseph Soloveitchik, a leader of Modern Orthodoxy, who had already rendered a more nuanced opinion on dialogue with Christians. Under his leadership, the Orthodox Rabbinical Council of America had issued a statement in 1964 that "endorsed Jewish-Christian dialogue on social and political issues of general human

concern," but ruled that members "were opposed to such dialogue on matters of faith."[14]

Although Orthodox communities do not represent the
majority of Jews in the United States, it is startling to encounter
such opposition to dialogue with Christians, especially after
Vatican II. It is sobering to find the opposition grounded in a
longstanding debate in Jewish tradition as to the status of
Christianity in the context of what constitutes idolatry.

In contrast, more positive modern Jewish views on the relationship of Judaism to other religions affirm religious pluralism. More liberal thinkers base their judgments in part on the
implications of *Tselem Elohim* (humans created in God's
image) found in Genesis 1:26. "Then," Rabbi Irving Greenberg
says, "any religion or culture that shows it can raise people in
the image of God can be criticized, corrected, even rejected, but
it deserves the consideration which comes after being heard."[15]
An Orthodox rabbi well known for his work on religious pluralism, Greenberg believes that his "truth/faith system cannot
fulfill God's dreams. Therefore, the world needs the contribution that the other makes for the world's own wholeness and
perfection."[16] The ideal of humans being created in God's
image, however, does not give license for humans to assume
full knowledge of God's will. Indeed, essential to any affirmation of pluralism is the recognition that we are limited in our
very humanness. As Elliott Dorff, a leading scholar in the
Conservative Movement, claims, "From the standpoint of
piety, pluralism emerges not from relativism, but from a deeply
held and aptly humble monotheism."[17]

Jews today do not necessarily agree with the rabbis and
medieval commentators who viewed Christianity as potentially
idolatrous. Nor is it likely they hold the pluralist positions of
Greenberg and Dorff. Rather, many Jews, who rely less on theology than on history to shape their views of other religions,
feel caught in a tension. On the one hand, they are attracted to

the humanistic view that all creatures deserve God's blessing. Yet they are mindful that those in other religious traditions, primarily Christianity but more recently Islam, may not warrant such a blessing because of how they have acted toward those of different faiths, especially Jews. Moreover, even liberal Jews may be wary of dialogue with Christians out of the fear that such engagement is really motivated by the desire to convert Jews. Memories of the Inquisition and other attempts by the Catholic Church to force conversion linger in the Jewish soul. Today, many Jews resent evangelical groups' attempts to convert them, that they might be "saved."

Saved and damned. Pure worship and idolatrous worship. Both Christianity and Judaism have made use of binary categories to deal with the religious other. Of course, many other religions also have adherents who look at the world from a similar binary understanding: Anyone whose system of belief and practice differs from ours is thereby an infidel, a nonbeliever. But persons need not remain—and indeed should not remain—in this limited perspective.

Barry Rosen, one of the fifty-two Americans held hostage in Iran from 1979 to 1980 who has since become very interested in Islamic culture, recounts an experience of expanding someone's religious horizons. As director of the Teachers College Afghanistan Project working with the Afghanistan Ministry of Education, Rosen was walking with some of his team members on a road in Kabul when they came upon a boy playing in an old Soviet tank. Rosen, who speaks Dari, began talking with him. Perhaps because of Rosen's language proficiency, the boy assumed he was a Muslim and referred to the other team members as *kafirs*, or nonbelievers. In response, Rosen explained that it was not that they were nonbelievers but rather that their religious beliefs differed from those of Muslims. He then invited the boy to talk to his team, asking each team member in turn whether he or she believed in a religion. Translating for the boy, Rosen reports that the boy was "fascinated to learn that all non-Muslims weren't also nonbelievers." For Rosen himself, "it was one of those rare moments where you feel you're making a difference, and you can actually see it happening."[18]

EDUCATING BEYOND TOLERANCE
FOR A TEXTURED PARTICULARISM

While our own adventures have generally taken place far closer to home and with more educated participants, we, too, have had moments when we felt we were making a difference in breaking down stereotypes and misconceptions. Yet, we desire to do more than contribute to greater tolerance of the religious other. Tolerance, however desirable and necessary, does not inevitably lead to understanding the other; it merely permits people to live alongside those who differ from them without demeaning them. Neither does tolerance require that they learn anything about the other. Pluralism, in contrast, demands pursuing understanding; it is built upon an encounter of commitments and a respect for difference that flows from knowledge of one's own tradition.[19] As religious educators, we want those with whom we work to *learn* about the religious other—and in so doing, also to learn something profound about their own tradition. Jean Halperin expresses an insight fundamental to our own work: "We not only need to understand one another, we need one another to understand ourselves."[20]

We situate our work under the rubric of religious pluralism, but from a distinctive angle. We believe that persons knowledgeable about and committed to their own religious tradition are best positioned to contribute to a religiously pluralistic society. We must, therefore, teach in ways that form a religious identity vibrant and learned enough to cross religious borders intelligently and sensitively. For us, this means forming persons in what we call a *textured particularism*: a keen sense of the beliefs and practices of one's own religious tradition as well as the finitude of that tradition. Our passion is to educate Jews and Christians in ways that "make a space" for the other, those "who sing a different song, hear a different music, tell a different story."

PARTICULARISM: TEXTURED, INSULAR, AND ADVERSARIAL

A *textured* particularism differs from an *insular* particularism, which we see as synonymous with parochialism: superficial, provincial, and religion-centric, if relatively benign. Many persons lack knowledge of religious traditions outside their own. This happens even within traditions themselves; for example, despite the ecumenical movement, many Christians are ill-informed about other denominations. Without knowledge of the religious "other," persons tend to project categories and concepts from their own tradition onto everyone else.

Adversarial particularism is a more dangerous form of particularism, because it diminishes, caricatures, or even demonizes the other. Ignorant of the other, it gives rise to bigotry and legitimates discrimination (e.g., white supremacist groups, the Taliban). An adversarial particularism rightly gives religion a bad name—but it ought not to be confused with a textured particularism that is rooted in the rich images, practices, symbols, and stories of one's religious traditions.

Our experience suggests that a textured particularism is relatively rare. Even within our religious traditions, many people lack an experience of the tradition's profundity. Banal liturgies, sporadic or inadequate religious education, and lack of familial involvement in the religious tradition inhibit development of a mature and textured religious identity. A rich and receptive particularism, in contrast, is necessary for developing a religious identity that is simultaneously rooted and adaptive,

grounded and ambiguous—that is, one that allows for engagement with the religious other.

A textured particularism is passionate. It implies deep, even
visceral connections to one's religious tradition. It requires a
serious immersion in the community's life—in those symbol-
rich moments in which the Divine Presence and the power of
the faith community are experienced. At the same time, the
requisite knowledge of one's tradition contributes to a profound humility about the tradition—the ways in which the
community of faith has been unfaithful to its vision of God.

In our time, a textured particularism must include knowing
about the religious other. "The test of faith is whether I can
make a space for difference," Rabbi Sacks writes.[21] The future
of our planet depends on it.

There are, of course, many religious "others" to know, and
the vast majority of us have neither the opportunity nor sufficient knowledge to engage all the religious traditions. Yet
knowing just one other religious tradition beyond one's own
offers a vast new horizon of understanding. And, in the case of
Christians and Jews, there is a distinctive relationship, both
theological and historical. Because our work has been with
these two peoples with a contentious, even tragic, history, we
have been privileged to participate in healing a divide.

JEWS AND CHRISTIANS: A COMPLICATED RELATIONSHIP

In vast sectors of the world, Christians have few opportunities
to know Jews personally. Despite the demographic realities
that limit contact (a high percentage of Jews live in only fourteen nations of the world), Judaism is not unknown to
Christians, since Christian origins are inextricably bound up in
Judaism. Two problems arise from this situation: Most
Christians think of Jews as the "Hebrews of old," and what

they know about Judaism is dependent on how they understand the complexities of Christian origins, which are often conveyed in simplistic ways.

For example, a friend of ours, now a prominent rabbi, tells the story of his frequent trips through the airport when he was a rabbinic student at the Cincinnati campus of Hebrew Union College. Sent to southern cities where rabbis were few in number so that he could lead services for holidays, he often brought religious artifacts with him, such as boxes of Tanakh (the Jewish Bible) or biblical commentaries. Over the years, he came to know some of the airport personnel, who were quite fascinated with this young Jew. On one of his last trips, his baggage included items needed to cook his congregants a Chinese dinner (our friend is a gourmet cook). "I know what this oil is for," one of the security agents said to him. "You need that for the animal sacrifice." Never mind that Jews haven't offered sacrifice since the destruction of the Second Temple in 70 C.E. What this security agent knew was her "Old" Testament, with its elaborate specification of ways in which sacrifices were to be offered. To her, Jews were the people who lived by the Old Testament.

Jewish stereotypes of Christians work in a different direction. Because knowledge of Christianity is not requisite for Jewish self-understanding, the broader culture mediates what most Jews understand about Christian teachings. In our time, the dominance of evangelicals on television and in the public sphere means that many Jews equate Christianity with the views of Pat Robertson or Jerry Falwell. Or, such as in Sara's experience of growing up in Irish-Catholic Boston, some Jews conflate Catholicism with Christianity. But however Jews understand Christianity, most associate it with centuries of hostility and hate. Antisemitism and Christianity are paired— and are seen by some as inseparable.

A painful memory illustrates this. Mary had been teaching a course, "Different Faces of God," with a Jewish woman in New York in an adult education course run by a Jewish agency. Most of the participants were Jews, though there was one Catholic and another with a Catholic background. Much of the course involved exploring differences and similarities in spirituality. During the session on key rituals and symbols, Mary showed how Christianity took up Passover imagery. Later in the evening, it was decided that as an optional exercise some course participants might see this imagery at play in the Holy Thursday liturgy of a local church.

The first scripture reading of the liturgy of Holy Thursday is taken from the account of the Passover in Exodus 12. This narrative gave rise to a layering of symbols among Jesus's followers, such as Paul's proclamation, "Christ our paschal lamb has been sacrificed" (1 Cor. 5:7). A dramatic ritual, based on the Gospel text of the day, accompanies the commemoration of the Last Supper:

> After he had washed their feet, had put on his robe, and had returned to the table, he said to them, "Do you know what I have done to you? You call me Teacher and Lord—and you are right, for that is what I am. So if I, your Lord and Teacher, have washed your feet, you also ought to wash one another's feet. For I have set you an example, that you also should do as I have done to you." (John 13:12–15)

It is the custom in this parish, after the priests and others with liturgical roles have washed the feet of selected participants, to invite others in the congregation to wash one another's feet. It continues for as long as congregants participate in the footwashing and is always very moving. Typically, during this time some version of the hymn "Ubi Caritas et Amor" is sung:

> *Ubi caritas et amor, Deus ibi est.*
> *Congregavit nos in unum Christi amor.*
> *Exultemus, et in ipso iucundemur.*
> *Timeamus, et amemus Deum vivum*
> *Et ex corde diligamus nos sincero.*

> Where holy and earthly love are, there is God.
> Christ's love has brought us into one.
> Let us rejoice in him
> and fear and love the living God
> and prize him above all things with our heart.

During the evening, other hymns were also sung emphasizing God's love.

Because it was late when the service ended, those who had been guests at this liturgy went their separate ways. At the next session of the course, Mary and her colleague opened with an opportunity for participants to respond to what they had experienced. One class member immediately launched into a tirade about the hypocrisy of Christians singing about love at their services, then going out and persecuting Jews. One would have thought that every congregant at this New York City parish went to church only to foster hatred toward Jews. Her vitriolic denunciation of her interpretation of the liturgy took everyone in the class aback. Apparently, that liturgy had evoked feelings that had been building for many years, yet had been covered over in the civility of previous sessions. It was a painful session.

In the split second that educators have to make decisions about interactions, Mary decided it was important simply to receive this person's emotions, so she did not move the discussion to a more analytical level. Yet Mary left the session deeply disturbed; even at more than a year's distance from that evening, she has mixed emotions. She understands that this woman must have still-tender wounds from her encounter with the church and with Christians (her Jewish colleague later debriefed her), yet knows that "dumping" her rage on the group undercut much of what the sessions had been designed to do—and unfairly maligned her parish.

JUDAISM AND CHRISTIANITY: A FUNDAMENTAL ASYMMETRY

Although in our work together we have often witnessed the expression of strong emotions, the intensity of this woman's outburst is atypical. Nevertheless, it vividly illustrates one of our fundamental convictions: When Jews are in the presence of Christians, history is always on the table. Jews build their identity as much on history as on core beliefs of tradition; history plays a central part in Jewish self-understanding. To a certain extent, from a Jewish perspective it is highly problematic that Christianity has its roots in Judaism. Without a proper understanding of symbol systems, it can appear that Christianity's use of central Jewish events and practices (e.g., Passover) eliminates or supersedes the original Jewish meanings—and many Christians have indeed regarded Judaism as a vestige of the past, the "promise" to their "fulfillment." Even if Jews today may not have *personally* experienced anti-semitism at Christian hands, they are acutely conscious of how Jews over the centuries have been disparaged and demeaned by the church—the Crusades, the Inquisition, the burnings of the Talmud, the ghettoes, the forced baptisms—and thus conclude that they can't have an honest, religiously grounded relationship with Christians until they face their history. The Shoah (Holocaust) stands as the preeminent question to Christians because it asks not only "Where were you?" but also "How could your tradition have for so many generations taught contempt for Jews?"

THE ASYMMETRY AT THE HEART OF OUR WORK

As we have worked together, we have come to understand a fundamental lack of symmetry in the agenda, as it were, of each tradition. For Christians, theology is the issue: How might they respect the integrity and profundity of Judaism while respecting and reverencing the centrality of Jesus Christ to the church? For Jews, history is the issue: How can they relate to, even reconcile with, a tradition that has caused them so much suffering over nearly two thousand years? The challenge for Jews, as Sara's colleague, Rabbi David Ellenson (now the president of Hebrew Union College) expressed it, is to come to understand "that Christianity meant and means more than the persecution of Jews. The Church, no matter how heinous its role in provoking anti-Jewish sentiment has been in the past, also has spoken to the religious and spiritual needs of those devoted to it."[22]

Addressing this asymmetry has become one of the cornerstones of our work together. Fundamental to our work is the conviction that each tradition must engage in a process of transformation, but that the nature of the transformation differs. Jews need to address their self-understanding based on history, and Christians need to reconstitute their theology because so much of it has been grounded in an inadequate understanding of Judaism. This is a complex matter, because in both cases we are dealing with issues that are buried deep in the religious identities of participants.

Moreover, because history overshadows the Jewish-Christian encounter, we have invited participants to study it in the presence of the other. In some cases, this has involved offering a more nuanced narrative of the complex, painful, and prolonged "partings of the ways" between our two communities in the early centuries of the Common Era. In other cases, we have traced the development of anti-Jewish teachings and

attitudes in Christianity, showing how such teachings and attitudes absorbed new layers over time, becoming ever more
deadly.[23] For the most part, Christian participants have not
known this horrific dimension of church history, and they
experience deep shame; Jewish participants, although surprised
that this history has not been part of Christian education, are
relieved by the horror their Christian counterparts express. As
one Jewish participant said after we had studied history
together, "Now we can get off the medieval battlefield."

Complicating this further is that Christianity's changing
theological understanding of Judaism—and, therefore, of
itself—makes many Jews wary. We can think of no better illus-
tration of this than a story another rabbi friend tells. Early in
his childhood, his parents divorced. Their acrimonious separation meant that the children had to negotiate difficult emotional matters. Yet, because this was the way things were, he
learned to deal with the realities. But then, after some twenty-
five years, his parents reconciled and remarried. However wonderful this might have been on many levels, our friend
experienced turmoil. He had known how to relate to each parent when they were one another's enemies, but not in this new
relationship as friend and spouse. So, too, he had known how
to relate to Christians when he could think of them as enemies
of the Jewish people. But now that many Christian denominations were taking responsibility for the tragic history of their
relationship with Judaism and were seeking to reconcile with
Jews, he felt confused and uneasy.

The analogy might be carried further: Judaism and
Christianity are not simply two religious traditions that have a
history of hostility, but one tradition has abused the other and
is now coming to terms with the consequences of this abuse. To
say that history is always on the table is to recognize that deep
wounds take a long time to heal and that those who seek to
help with the healing must be both skilled and sensitive.

The chapters that follow describe some of our attempts to help with this healing through education. We believe passionately in the power of education to transform, especially when priority is given to processes and resources that develop and build upon the interaction of participants. From the start of our first extended work together, at the Catholic-Jewish Colloquium, which began in 1993, we have premised our work on what we came to term *interreligious learning*: study in the presence of the other and encounter with the tradition embodied in the other. Our goal is to transcend learning about the other in the abstract, as important as that may be, in order to have participants encounter Judaism or Christianity as it is lived by informed and committed Jews and Christians.[24]

The sort of transformation we aim for in our educational work does not happen overnight. What we hope is that a seed has been planted and that the resources, framework, and opportunities we have developed provide sufficient nurture for the flourishing of new attitudes and understandings.

Before describing our educational adventures, however, we first provide some personal background—because our differences enrich our mutual work.

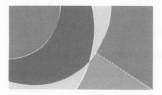

2

SARA'S STORY

In August 2004 I found myself in a car traveling from Krakow, Poland, to the Auschwitz concentration camp. For a Jew who is also a Jewish educator to be making this pilgrimage might not seem unusual at first. What made this journey unique was my companion—a longtime Catholic friend and colleague.

Mary Boys, a member of the Sisters of the Holy Names of Jesus and Mary and a professor at Union Theological Seminary, had urged me to go to Auschwitz with her as a natural outgrowth of our work. I saw it as an important step in my ongoing journey as a Jew and as a powerful learning experience about how the Holocaust affects the relationship and discourse between Jews and Christians. Mary's and my work together has shown that the Holocaust is both a historical reality and a difficult issue frequently present—spoken or unspoken—when Jews and Christians come together. This is especially true for those generations of Jews such as mine for whom confronting the Holocaust in our upbringing and religious education was especially significant.

The distance, however, from a Jewish childhood and youth in Boston to visiting Auschwitz with a Catholic friend, a nun, is almost unimaginable. As a parent, a grandparent, and an academic in Jewish education, I have a reputation as a meticulous planner. Yet there is no way that I could have foreseen or planned my engagement with Jewish-Catholic interreligious learning or my deep relationship and enduring collaboration with Mary Boys.

I grew up during the 1940s and 1950s in Boston, a city whose own story places mine in important historical context. There were, on the one hand, substantial pockets of immigrants and their young offspring who were first-generation Americans. My father was born in Russia. My mother, born in Boston, was the daughter of Russian immigrants. Most of my peers had two immigrant parents. At the same time, the post–World War II boom allowed veterans who otherwise might not have gone to college to take advantage of the G.I. Bill, which supported their higher education. As Jews, among others, gained a college education and began to move up the professional ladder, they also began to move from the city to the suburbs, which brought them into contact with non-Jews on a daily basis.

Yet my most formative years took place solely in Boston's urban core, where I had little contact with non-Jews until high school. That is the reality I seek to describe. It is a very different one from that of two of my grandchildren, who have grown up in Newton, a heavily Jewish Boston suburb. Although they have had intensive Jewish educational experiences, they routinely share as much with their non-Jewish neighbors and peers as they do with their fellow Jews.

To explain my Boston upbringing in context, I want to acknowledge its profound sense of history, beginning with the Colonial period, and how Bostonians have perceived themselves as the vanguard of America's pursuit of its destiny.

Through the city's magnetism for many immigrant groups, large numbers of Irish, Italians, and Jews arrived there to create new and different lives. Their experiences were often colored by the prominence and influence of the Yankee aristocracy—the Boston Brahmins—who tended to look down on both Catholics and Jews.

Arnold Band, a scholar of modern Hebrew literature, describes growing up in Boston in the 1930s and 1940s. Although the history and culture of Boston were always in the background, he recalls:

> In our personal lives, we were affected more by the mundane Boston of the streets, the tensions between its various ethnic groups; the long entrenched white Protestant elite, the "WASPS"; the well organized masses of Irish Catholics who had wrested political, but not financial power from the WASP establishment by the latter decades of the nineteenth century; the Sicilian laborers and peddlers concentrated in the North End and East Boston; and, of course, our Jews, scattered in many areas, but centered in our parts of Mattapan, Dorchester, and Roxbury.[1]

Growing up I was aware of this aristocracy, although I had no interaction with it until I arrived at Radcliffe College as a young adult. What affected my earlier years were the tensions between the immigrant groups, all attempting to move up the social and economic ladder. In particular, there is a documented history of the tensions between Catholics and Jews in Boston.[2] Although I cannot recall overtly hostile acts toward me, either physical or verbal, my memory may have become fuzzy over the years in this regard. Yet I do believe that the overall urban environment contributed to a diffuse anxiety about Catholics because they appeared so omnipresent and colored the city's cultural environment. It certainly led to my feeling like an outsider, even as I lived in an overwhelmingly Jewish neighborhood. I later learned that my experience with these tensions was very different from that of my younger brother.

In my youth and young adulthood, the Catholic Church was overwhelming to me. I probably naively thought that Catholics were the majority in the world. In part this was because I grew up in neighborhoods adjacent to where many Catholics lived, although I had no social contact with them. It is only through my later experiences that I learned that Catholics, like Jews, were a minority in the midst of the country's much larger Protestant population. I also learned that Catholics struggled with the meaning of their immigrant status, needing, as Jews did, to adapt to the new social, economic, and religious realities of America.

In Roxbury, where I grew up, the majority of my neighbors were Jews. On the major Jewish holidays in this organic Jewish community, the streets were filled with Jews. Children and young teens frequently lingered outside the synagogues, rather than worshipping inside. Growing up in this overwhelming Jewish environment, being Jewish was part of the air we breathed, part of the rhythm of life, a cultural and an ethnic identity. It was not just a religious tradition. We took being Jewish for granted and did not think that religious worship was the only way we could mark our Jewish identity. The reality that Judaism is a cultural, national, and ethnic identity is often hard for people from other faith traditions to understand. For me, the in-depth exploration of Judaism as a religious tradition would come during young adulthood rather than during my youth in Roxbury.

Arnold Band's comment about the Irish-Catholic political power in Boston underscores my early sense that the Catholic Church was extremely important in the community, even if

Catholics were a minority. This colored my experience growing up. I felt on the margins, not because of the Brahmins, with whom I had no contact, but because of the pervasive Catholic culture and the power Catholics seemed to exercise. My feelings and relationship to this Catholic presence would best be characterized as somewhere between alienation and anxiety. The irony is that they were not based on any knowledge of Christianity in general or Catholicism in particular. More important, I had no social contact with Catholics my own age until I reached secondary school, and there we did not really socialize outside of school. Through my subsequent life and interreligious experiences I have learned the ultimate importance of interpersonal relationships in humanizing the religious other.

My elementary education took place in an overwhelmingly Jewish neighborhood, with mostly Irish-Catholic teachers. The religious background of the teachers was largely irrelevant, however, given the elementary school's location in a Jewish area and its predominately Jewish student body. However, my younger brother shared with me his concern about a possible undertone of anti-Jewish sentiment, expressed in subtle and strange ways.

One example revolved around the celebration of Christmas. In a school whose student body was 90 percent Jewish, there was a requirement for students to participate in a choir whose annual Christmas concert comprised only carols. When our mother, a woman who never hesitated to speak her mind, objected to the practice in a conversation with the principal, she was told that she could simply remove my brother from the choir.

I moved from this school to Girls' Latin School when I entered the seventh grade. Girls' Latin, which introduced me to a more religiously diverse setting, was a highly selective public school that offered only a rigorous academic track, modeled on the private New England preparatory schools. Students had to take six years of Latin and two other foreign languages in addition to the traditional disciplines. Acceptance was based on elementary school grades. Students came from all parts of the city, so most—myself included—had to travel long distances by public transportation. This made after-school socializing difficult to impossible.

In reading about the city's tensions that coincided with my years at Girls' Latin, I am surprised that I have no memory of being threatened by other young people going to and from school.[3] I attribute that to the prevailing cultural norm that girls were not to be the target of physical threats.

At Girls' Latin School, I encountered girls from across the religious spectrum and, once again, teachers who were largely Irish-Catholic. In the environment of Girls' Latin, the religious identity of the teachers affected the culture of the school, and as was the case in elementary school, particularly around Christmas.

Although I encountered no antisemitism on the part of either teachers or fellow students, the environment as Christmas approached was alienating. The choir practiced Christmas carols with clear religious messages. Almost no notice was taken of the large number of Jewish students for whom this was intensely marginalizing. The fact was that in Boston, in a school where the faculty was mainly Irish-Catholic, Christmas was a serious religious holiday. Santa Claus, the concept of multicultural winter solstice observances, and Chanukah had no place. I am still aware of how much I dreaded the approach of this season and how much it reinforced my sense of being an outsider. It is interesting that on my visits to Boston at Christmastime to visit my daughter and her family, the familiar sights of electric candles and Christmas trees in the windows generate some of those old feelings of being an outsider with much greater strength than I have ever felt while living in Los Angeles.

It is important to state that at Girls' Latin, teachers' relationships with students were based only on academic performance. Neither religion nor race was a variable in their views of students. Each student's academic potential was the critical factor.

In my six years at Girls' Latin, my bond with fellow students was forged primarily around our mountains of homework, the rigor of the tests we had to take, and our worries about staying the course there as we watched many of our classmates fall by the wayside and have to return to their neighborhood schools. We did not engage in any real conversations about religion, and I would have been ill-equipped to do so. My home was nominally Jewish in that we belonged to a synagogue but observed few rituals. My Jewish education was very sparse, but my Jewish identity, nurtured by my neighborhood and my grandparents, was strong. Growing up as I did in an environment that was ethnically and culturally Jewish, I was secure in my Jewish identity and proud of it, even if I was not well-grounded in the beliefs and practices of Judaism as a religion.

My younger brother had a very different experience growing up in Boston. He described it to me as a version of "West Side Story," only the protagonists in this case were Jewish boys, aged nine to fifteen, from Roxbury and Dorchester, and Irish-Catholic boys from nearby Hyde Park.[4] My brother related that he was occasionally beaten when the Irish-Catholic boys would invade the Jewish neighborhood, particularly around Jewish holidays. His experiences are similar to those documented and described by Goldstein in her thesis on Jews and Catholics in Boston:

> According to Hecht House reports, chronicling the attacks, antisemitism occurred in various places: occasionally Irish boys burst into the community center; Irish-Catholic youth also waited outside the house; others experienced antisemitism at Dorchester High

School. There were at least nineteen reported incidents between July 1943 and September 1943.[5]

My brother described his experience, which took place around that same time and continued until the early 1950s, as quite violent, and he reported that Jewish youth mobilized to retaliate. The attacks on Jewish boys by the Irish-Catholic gangs were accompanied by antisemitic rhetoric and included the use of bats, broken bottles, switchblade knives, and chains. In one of those incidents, my brother was injured and was taken to a hospital. The "Jewish gangs" of boys like the one my brother belonged to would seek vengeance by invading the Hyde Park neighborhood with implements to hurt the "Irish-Catholic gang" that had attacked them. These incidents ceased as more and more Jews moved out of the area and more African-Americans moved in.

My brother's basic mistrust of all Christians throughout college and graduate school illustrates the lasting effects of such encounters and the prejudice they produce. Only encounters with some Christians who embraced him as a Jew when he was appointed to a faculty position at the University of North Carolina at Chapel Hill provided some counterpoint to his childhood experiences. The irony, of course, is that among those who embraced him there was, more than likely, the belief that my brother could never achieve salvation as a Jew. For example, the Southern Baptist Convention—the largest Protestant denomination in the United States, with some fifteen million members, and dominant in the South, where my brother lives—pledged at its June 1996 convention to "direct prayers, energies and resources toward converting Jews."[6] The significance of my brother's story is that it indicates how a childhood in the environment in which we grew up could make it unthinkable that a Jew would eventually choose to engage in interreligious work with Catholics.

FROM THE PERIPHERY TO THE CENTER

Although my engagement with Judaism as a religion was somewhat superficial, a series of events, beginning with my junior year in high school, altered the course of my life forever. At the invitation of a male friend, I attended a meeting of Young Judaea, a Zionist youth group in which high school students gathered regularly to study Zionism and to develop a relationship with the infant State of Israel, founded in 1948. It was here that I encountered a brilliant Harvard graduate student, Arnold Band, who acted as the leader of this particular group. The discussions were very serious. We read and discussed the great thinkers and founders of Zionism.[7] As I was drawn into this circle of serious young Jews who were passionate about Zionism and Israel, I became involved with Young Judaea, met my future husband, and began to shape a Jewish identity that has influenced the rest of my life and that of my family.

When I graduated from Girls' Latin School in 1950 and entered Radcliffe College, I immersed myself not only in my studies but also in Jewish activity on campus at Harvard Hillel. At the same time I continued my activities with Young Judaea, attending national conventions and leading a group of younger members. Because I commuted to Radcliffe, I did not develop a circle of friends, which would have enhanced my understanding of other religious faiths. I also suspect that in the liberal environment of Harvard-Radcliffe few students would have declared themselves overtly religious. My social circle grew ever narrower, comprising highly motivated college students who took their Judaism and Zionism very seriously. Reflecting back, quite a few of my male friends from this period became rabbis and eventually moved to Israel.

In February 2005 I had a reunion with one of those rabbis in Jerusalem, and we reminisced about the intense Jewish/Zionist experience we had experienced at Harvard Hillel. During that period, although the city of Boston had not changed and tensions still existed, I no longer thought much about the Catholics around me. Beyond my studies at Harvard-Radcliffe, my commitments to Young Judaea and Harvard Hillel now occupied most of my time and my interests. I was now fully engaged with and grounded in my own religious particularism.[8]

In the fall semester of my second year in college, I received an invitation that was to shape my future and that of my family in profound ways. Through Young Judaea, I was offered a scholarship for a year-long program in the State of Israel. The Institute for Youth Leaders from Abroad of the Jewish Agency for Israel invites selected leaders from Zionist youth movements throughout the world to study in Israel in order to prepare them to educate and lead members of their youth movement in their home communities.[9] I received a one-year leave of absence from Radcliffe College and left for a year of experiences (1952–1953) that would prove challenging, both physically and emotionally. This involved a program of study that taught me the Hebrew language, Jewish history, and the evolution of Zionism and the modern State of Israel. Yet even my background and education in Young Judaea did not prepare me for what I encountered.

In 1953, Israel as a Jewish state was only five years old and was absorbing multitudes of immigrants from many countries, although it had neither the economy nor the infrastructure to accomplish this. What Israel did have was the pioneering spirit, the dedication, and the sheer will to fulfill its destiny as the homeland for the Jewish people.[10] This was a very difficult time to be living in Israel, especially for a young American who took many physical comforts for granted. Although we lived for half a year in Jerusalem, where we studied, Jerusalem was at the time a divided city. In fact, the geography of Israel at that time was such that on many occasions when we traveled we had to be careful not to attract enemy gunfire from a nearby border. I have many powerful memories of encountering biblical history in this land, of working the fields of a kibbutz (a collective farming settlement), of meeting for the first time Holocaust survivors beginning a new life, of feeling the pride of living in a country where the holidays were those of the Jewish calendar and where Jewish culture marked everyday life.

I recall celebrating Passover on a kibbutz in the Galilee, where the Seder not only recounted the story of the Exodus but also marked the agricultural significance of the festival that we could see in the fields around us. My kibbutz period was spent at *Ein Tsurim*, a religious kibbutz that had originally been located outside Jerusalem and was destroyed by the Jordanian legion in the War for Independence in 1948. Survivors of that kibbutz built a new one with the same name south of Tel Aviv, but the events of the War for Independence were part of the living memory of everyone there.

These experiences and memories were far from anything I could have imagined when I was growing up as a Jew in Boston. Israel allowed me to feel what it is like to be the majority, not the marginalized. Being in Israel meant living in a national culture that was Jewish, an experience that can take place only in Israel. That year allowed me to grow in my self-confidence as a Jew and planted in me a love and engagement with Israel that to this day is at the core of my personal Jewish identity.

My experience in Israel also brought me face to face with the reality that this land was the Holy Land for Christians as well. At the time, I did not fully appreciate what that meant, but I do recall one of our *tiyulim* (extended hikes) that brought us to *Kfar Nachum* (Capernaeum). This is an ancient synagogue site associated with Jesus, which in a concrete way demonstrated that this land was also the home to Jesus and his followers. We did not have access to the Old City of Jerusalem, which would have heightened our awareness of the deep connections of Christians to this place, and of Muslims as well. At that particular time in my life, I must admit, I could not have truly appreciated those connections because I did not have any real Christian friends, nor had I engaged in any serious study about the origins of Christianity.

In light of my earlier negative feelings about the approach of Christmas, I was struck by an incident outside the YMCA in Jerusalem. My fellow students and I were barely aware that Christmas was approaching when one night we noticed a large Christmas tree in the window of the YMCA. Drawn to it by our experiences in our home countries, we approached the window in time to hear a young Israeli child ask his father in Hebrew, *"Abba, mah zeh?"* (Dad, what is that?) We were struck by the vast difference between Jews growing up in a country where Jewish culture is the majority culture and Jews growing up in the Jewish Diaspora as minorities in an essentially Christian culture. Perhaps in that moment the seed of resolve was planted for my striving to raise and educate Jews with a sense of pride in who they are, regardless of their minority status.

My experience in Israel during that year was formative. Both personally and professionally, Israel has been a major part of my self-understanding as a Jew. It has also been a significant impetus in my work as a Jewish educator, for which I have been honored twice by the State of Israel. In June 1997 I received the Samuel Rothberg Prize for Jewish Education, awarded by Hebrew University in Jerusalem. As I sat on the stage of the amphitheater on Mount Scopus, I could not believe that I was the same person who had first encountered Israel in its infancy, when access to Mount Scopus was not possible for Jews. The drama of that moment did not escape me.

When I received a call in November 2004 that I was to receive the *Pras HaNasi*, the President's Award for Jewish Education in the Diaspora, I was overwhelmed. Standing before the President of the State of Israel on February 21, 2005, in the presence of my students, friends, and colleagues, to receive the prize from his hands was one of the most emotional moments in my life. Helping Christian dialogue partners to understand how deeply I and other Jews feel connected to the Land of Israel is of paramount importance for me.

PHYSICAL AND SPIRITUAL JOURNEYS

During my senior year at Radcliffe, I married the man I met through Young Judaea, and we set about creating our life together. David entered medical school, and after graduation I worked at the Hillel Foundation at Boston University. The next step in our lives involved leaving Boston and moving to Cleveland for his surgical internship. With our infant daughter Aviva, we decided to live in a garden apartment in a nearby suburb. From many points of view, including its distance from the hospital where David was on call every other night, this was a bad decision. Yet it would turn out to be fortuitous in terms of my building a relationship with Catholics. Left alone much of the time, without friends and family, I was welcomed by two families on the same floor. Each had one young child and each was devoutly Catholic. They became my family during that long, cold year, and they invited me to be a part of their family life and celebrations. Sharing in their Christmas radically changed my feelings toward the holiday. I grew to appreciate their faith and their dedication to their church. These two families gave a face and a reality to Catholicism that allowed me to begin to analyze my past feelings and to think about Catholicism in new ways. This friendship was also important because these two families had never encountered a knowledgeable and committed Jew.

In a very informal way, this was my introduction to dialogue between Catholics and Jews. Although we seldom discussed theology, we shared our understanding of the rituals and culture of our two traditions, and we did so as friends. Later, in my work with Mary Boys, the importance of friendship in building bridges between people of faith would become even more self-evident.

The next fourteen years brought about many changes in our lives. We spent three years in the Air Force on bases in Virginia and Arizona, where we met fellow Air Force officers of many different faiths, but where religion was seldom discussed. Our son Joseph was born during this period, and we eventually settled in Los Angeles, where David completed his residency in urology. As we considered Los Angeles as our future home, we became involved in a synagogue, and I went back to teaching in congregational schools and continued to study Hebrew and Judaism in a program designed for religious school teachers. Our third child, Josh, was born shortly before the Six-Day War in Israel. I have vivid memories of pushing his baby carriage with a radio in my hand, wondering what Israel's fate would be. So when Hadassah, the organization that had sponsored my youth movement, Young Judaea, sought my involvement in building a youth movement and camping program in Southern California, I became an enthusiastic volunteer.[11] I devoted the next six years to the task with much success. This meant that my own children repeated the youth experience that had brought David and me together. Each one, in his or her own time, participated in groups, went to the movement camps, both locally and nationally, and eventually spent a summer and a year in Israel sponsored by Young Judaea.[12]

In 1973, to celebrate Joseph's bar mitzvah, we took all our children to Israel. This trip grew out of our enthusiasm after David and I participated in a Hadassah Medical Mission to Israel, as well as our desire to introduce our children to Israel, a place that meant so much to us. On the Hadassah trip we were able to visit parts of the country that had been inaccessible prior to 1967. For the first time we entered the Old City of Jerusalem, filled with history and sites sacred to Christians, Jews, and Muslims. In addition to visits to the Dome of the Rock and the Western Wall, we visited the many churches in the Old City, including the Church of the Holy Sepulchre, and walked the Via Dolorosa. What had been a mere impression of the sanctity of the Land of Israel for all three religions, which I had gained during my year of study in Israel, became a reality at these holy sites. At the time I did not fully realize the complexities that arise from the juxtaposition of the history of these three religions in this one, small sacred space and the implications for how the modern State of Israel is viewed from the different perspectives.

On my many visits to Israel since 1973 I have visited many other Christian sites, such as those in the Galilee, and continue to appreciate the ways in which the Land of Israel connects Jews and Christians, yet divides them because of the different meanings we ascribe to this land.

Indeed, the love of Israel that I felt and continue to feel, a love that is national and ethnic as well as religious, would prove to be difficult to explain to my Christian dialogue partners. As politics began to play an important role in the posture toward Israel for both Jews and Christians, the differing perspectives often led not only to conflicting ideas but also to tensions between individual Christians and Jews and their respective communities and leaders.[13]

STARTING LIFE ANEW:
CHALLENGES AND OPPORTUNITIES

In October 1974, David suffered a fatal heart attack and suddenly our lives were totally overturned. After the initial shock, the children went back to their schooling and I continued my volunteer work with Hadassah and our synagogue. Wondering how to reconstruct my own life led me to a decision that created a future I never could have imagined. The first step was a decision to enroll in a full-time M.A. program in Jewish Education at Hebrew Union College (HUC). With that step, I moved from religious education as my avocation to Jewish education as my profession. This decision brought me to the Rhea Hirsch School of Education as a student, where directly after graduation I became a member of its staff and in 1980 became its director, when the founding director stepped down for health reasons. Joining the faculty at HUC proved to be a major turning point in my interreligious journey.

Three encounters in my HUC experience created the building blocks for my subsequent work in interreligious learning for Catholics and Jews. Rabbi Michael J. Signer was a young member of the faculty when I arrived as a student. He was a medieval historian with great interest in the interaction between Christianity and Judaism, not only in the historical context of his specialty but also as it manifested itself in contemporary realities. Studying with him, then learning with him as a faculty colleague, allowed me to understand the complexity of this interaction in new ways. His prodigious knowledge of Christianity, as well as of Judaism, was a gift he brought to every encounter.

In studying medieval Jewish history with Michael, I began my first serious study of Christianity and the New Testament. As a student, I wrote my major research paper on "The Attitude of Paul the Apostle to the Law: An Analysis of the Epistles to Galatians and Romans in the Light of Paul's Religious and Philosophical Environment."[14] I also selected the Epistle of Barnabas as one of the three texts I analyzed for the final examination in that course.[15]

My second encounter of importance was the graduate study of Judaism at HUC. I emerged with a more sophisticated understanding of Jewish history and thought; the tools with which to study primary Jewish texts in Hebrew; and knowledge of the theological underpinnings of Jewish belief, practice, and values. All of that gave me confidence in my ability to analyze Judaism from a historical and scholarly perspective and to teach it and explain it with integrity to others. Without this confidence I do not think I could have ventured into the interreligious field with any sense of security. I emphasize this point because in my work with Mary we have learned how deep knowledge and the ability to answer difficult questions about one's own religious tradition are prerequisites for any probing conversations that Jews and Christians might have with one another.

When I assumed faculty responsibility and the directorship of the Rhea Hirsch School of Education, I came into contact with a program I did not know about when I was a student. HUC was one of the seminaries in California that participated in an Interseminary Retreat ("Intersem") for students. Initially, I knew only that it was sponsored by the National Conference of Christians and Jews (NCCJ) and that HUC rabbinical students were invited to attend along with seminarians from the University of Judaism (Conservative Judaism) and from Christian seminaries of all denominations. Michael Signer pointed out to me the importance of this program and suggested that students in the Rhea Hirsch School, who were preparing to be Jewish religious educators, would also benefit from the interaction with future religious leaders of different faiths.

Within a short time I began to serve on the planning committee for Intersem and chaired one of the annual events. My own education students began to attend as a result of my interest and urging. Intersem became not only a place where I entered into serious dialogue with future religious leaders from many faiths but also a model of the kind of interreligious encounter that should be made available to people of all faiths. It was at Intersem that I attended my first Catholic Mass and divested myself of fears as I came to appreciate its beauty and resonance with Jewish worship. I encountered Catholic seminarians, and I also became friends with a number of the priests who served as faculty at nearby St. John's Seminary in Camarillo.

I now realize that all of these steps were the crossing of a final boundary where I could begin to know something about Catholicism and appreciate it on its own terms. During this period I was honored by the National Conference of Christians and Jews for my contribution to the development of Intersem. Although the NCCJ is known today as the National Conference for Community and Justice, it continues the important work of bringing future religious leaders together through Intersem.[16]

As a result of my involvement with the NCCJ and Intersem, I was invited to design a project whereby students studying to be Jewish educators or rabbis would serve as guest faculty in Catholic high schools to teach about Judaism. The purpose of this project was to ensure that Catholic students would have an ongoing relationship with the guest faculty member who taught once a week in each school and would learn about Judaism from a knowledgeable and committed contemporary Jew. The first student to assume this role was Cynthia Reich, a graduate student in the Rhea Hirsch School, who received her Master of Arts in Jewish Education in 1984 and now serves as the director of the St. Paul Talmud Torah Day School in Minnesota. Cynthia traveled weekly to both Louisville High School in the San Fernando Valley, west of Los Angeles, and Ramona Convent Secondary School in the San Gabriel Valley, east of Los Angeles.[17]

Designing this program, supervising Cynthia Reich, including site visits to the two schools, and ensuring the continuity of the program were invaluable learning experiences for me. Among other things, I realized the importance of learning about a faith tradition from someone within that faith community. Since 1984, this program of Jewish religious leaders teaching in Catholic high schools has expanded to Catholic religious leaders teaching in Jewish high schools. The program is now a national program under the auspices of the American Jewish Committee and has reached more than 10,000 students in the Catholic-Jewish Educational Enrichment Program (C-JEEP).

NEXT STEPS IN THE JOURNEY

The most significant development in my journey was my encounter with Mary Boys on the porch of the Institute for Pastoral Ministry at Boston College in April 1985. I was there to convince her to be the guest scholar at an Interseminary Faculty Retreat in California. From such an inauspicious beginning evolved a twenty-year collaboration and my entry into a new world of interreligious study. I was already a member of the Religious Education Association (REA), but my work with Mary drew me into a deeper level of commitment, including membership on the board and sharing the chairmanship of the search committee for a new editor for the journal *Religious Education*. By the early 1990s I had cowritten two papers with Mary, which we presented at annual conferences of the Association of Professors and Researchers in Religious Education (APRRE) and published in *Religious Education*.[18]

Although REA had a number of Jewish members, APRRE had very few. As I attended more and more APRRE conferences, I became more comfortable with being on the periphery. At the annual Women's Luncheon, where every person talked about her work, I was often the only Jewish member in the room. Yet I was determined to remain in APRRE and involve more Jewish education academics. In this effort I was only moderately successful, for Jewish educators are overwhelmingly concerned with nurturing a distinctive Jewish identity for their students. They do not regard that identity as exclusively religious, but also cultural and ethnic. Conversations with educators of other faiths appear interesting, but not necessarily relevant to the challenge that Jewish educators perceive they are facing. Although I went on to be the first Jewish president of

APRRE and remain a member, my involvement over the past several years has not been substantial. My involvement with APRRE was, however, an important growth experience, contributing to my expanding knowledge of other faiths and their educational questions and issues.

REFLECTIONS ON THE JOURNEY

In retrospect, my experiences, rather than any ideology, have led me to serious engagement with the educational challenge of bridging the gap—and at times the chasm—between Christians and Jews. It is all too easy as a Jew to regard Christianity as Judaism gone astray and to believe that Judaism as a complete religion has little to learn from Christianity. On an emotional level, it is also difficult to divest oneself of the historic anger, fear, and sense of victimization in light of Christian anti-Jewish teachings and persecution over the centuries at the hands of the church. Furthermore, as a Jewish minority in a country where Christianity has historically held a privileged place, the challenge has been to preserve Jewish identity and not be absorbed into a national culture that has Christian roots. As I write, Jews and other minority faiths are anxious about the fundamentalist Christian rhetoric that is pervading our national discourse. Finally, for Jews who are deeply committed to Israel's survival, even as they disagree with certain political stances in Israel, it is disheartening to confront the anti-Israel sentiment of many segments of Christianity in America.

For all these reasons, a commitment to bringing Jews and Christians together, to acknowledging but transcending our difficult history, and to educating for religious pluralism and an appreciation of the religious other seem to be low priorities for a Jewish educator dedicated to building the Jewish future. In fact, such commitments are not widespread among Jewish educators. Given the length of my journey to this interreligious work, and how much of my growth in this area has been the result of twists of fate, I do sometimes ponder how I could have arrived at this place.

I believe that some stops along my journey, whether by accident or by choice, have been particularly significant. Without the relationship with my Catholic neighbors in Cleveland, I would not have appreciated the importance of friendship and hospitality in overcoming the fear and stereotypes I had about Catholics and Catholicism. That experience demonstrates to me that such feelings can be overcome. Without my experiences in Israel, where I could see for myself what it means for Jews to be in the majority and have power over their own destiny, I would have continued to be locked into a minority mind-set in the United States. Such a mind-set inhibits meaningful interreligious dialogue with Christians, who are the majority and therefore are perceived to be in a power relationship to Jews. Finally, my studies at HUC and beyond have provided me with a sophisticated understanding of my own Jewish tradition that is essential if I am to speak from a textured particularism as a Jew with people grounded in their own religious traditions.

I also wonder what sustains and drives me in this work. One conviction I now hold is that engaging on a deep level with committed Christians, particularly Catholics, has helped me grow in my own theology and develop new insight into my own Judaism. This engagement is like a mirror in which I see myself in a new light, which would not be accessible to me without the reflection in the image and faith of the other. My passion for this work seems like a natural outgrowth of trying to educate Jews to live in a pluralistic world. As I go forward, I believe that I am better able to teach my own children and grandchildren, as well as my students, to appreciate on a deep level that people of faith, whatever their tradition, carry out God's work in the world and embody *Tselem Elohim*, the image of God.

3

MARY'S STORY

Over the years I have often been asked how I came by my interest in and passion for Christian-Jewish relations. "By fits and starts" is one reply—and the most accurate.[1] My professional collaboration and friendship with Sara Lee are contributing factors, as is my schooling. Beyond those factors, however, lies a kaleidoscope of experiences and interests colored by chronological, geographical, and cultural overlays.

Let me begin with the overlays. I belong to the "baby boomer" generation, which for a Catholic meant growing up in the church of the Latin Mass. Steeped in the realms of ritual—Gregorian chant, processions, and May altars—we were schooled in the certainties of the *Baltimore Catechism*. Justly known for its didacticism, the *Baltimore Catechism*, written in 1885 and revised in 1941, reflects its origins in late nineteenth-century theology—a time when the church understood itself "over against" the world, particularly against what were perceived as "liberal" movements. The *Baltimore Catechism* serves as a marker of my generation. Ask any Catholic of similar background, "What is a sacrament?" and we will all respond without hesitation, "A sacrament is an outward sign instituted by Christ to give grace." The catechism contributed to our basic knowledge of the church's teachings and thereby provided a foundation on which we might develop more adequate understandings. Yet it also had liabilities: We memorized many answers to questions we did not have. Its theological defects were even more serious. Consider the following question and answer:

> **Q.** Why did the Jewish religion, which up to the death of Christ had been the true religion, cease at that time to be the true religion?
>
> **A.** The Jewish religion, which up to the death of Christ had been the true religion, ceased at that time to be the true religion because it was only a promise of the redemption and figure of the Christian religion, and when the redemption was accomplished and the Christian religion established by the death of Christ, the promise and figure were no longer necessary.[2]

In truth, I don't remember studying this question and answer; I discovered it about twenty years ago while paging through the catechism in order to teach about the evolution of Catholic educational thought.[3] Perhaps our class never advanced to later sections of the catechism. Nor would we have easily memorized the long, awkward answer. Moreover, I suspect our teachers had little curiosity about Christianity's relationship with Judaism, because the Jewish population at that time in Seattle, where I grew up, was small. Learning that Christianity had made Judaism obsolete was not nearly as important as being able to refute the more numerous Protestants. In my elementary school days, the Catholic Church's vocabulary had not yet expanded to include ecumenism or interreligious dialogue.

If the catechism's perspective on Judaism had little effect on me, it nonetheless provides a snapshot of the theology that suffused church life prior to Vatican II. The solemn liturgy of Good Friday included a prayer for the "perfidious Jews" until Pope John XXIII removed the phrase in 1959. Texts presented the Old Testament as mere promise, the New Testament as its fulfillment. Sermons suggested that the Gospels' depiction of legalistic Pharisees represented the emptiness of Judaism at the time of Jesus. Our formation in faith entailed a disparagement of Judaism, even if it avoided (as did mine) maligning Jews as "Christ-killers." Of course, our world included Muslims, Buddhists, Hindus, and a host of other religious peoples, but they were too exotic to figure into our parochial religious landscape. At any rate, the catechism informed us, "true religion was not universal before the coming of Christ. It was confined to one people—the descendants of Abraham. All other nations worshiped false gods."[4]

Despite the negative perspective on other religious traditions, we gained a rich sense of Catholic identity through ritual, symbol, and story that complemented the propositions of the catechism and compensated in large measure for its dry didacticism. It is clear, nonetheless, that our religious identity was formed in part *over against* the religious other, all of whom conveniently fit under the rubric "non-Catholic." Only Catholics, we were told from the pulpit and in the classroom, "had" the "true" faith.

Yet the realities of family and neighborhood often undermined the theological absolutes presented to us with such assurance. The catechism's claim that Judaism was no longer a true religion could not compete with the positive associations I already had with Judaism, thanks to our close family friend Pauline Lee. Pauline was a Jew who—most impressive to me—owned a candy store and came to our family celebrations with all manner of samples! On a more profound level, her friendship with three generations of our family implicitly taught me about accepting differences. Although my maternal grandfather was not religiously affiliated, my grandmother was actively involved in Catholic life in Seattle, and three of her four children (including my mother) were lifelong, practicing Catholics. None seemed to have had the slightest thought of converting Pauline, despite the theology of the time.

My father, a gracious, good, and gentle man, had no religious affiliation, so implicitly he offered another challenge to absolutist theological claims. He has thus played an important role in my thinking about belief and salvation. One of my few distinct memories as a first-grader is the sure knowledge that my teacher, whom I otherwise adored, was wrong in asserting that "only Catholics went to heaven." I could never believe in a heaven that would not include my father. As I continue to ponder today the meaning of salvation in Christian theology, I am grateful for the cognitive dissonance instigated in my childhood by the various neighbors, family members, and friends of moral integrity who belonged to other Christian denominations—or none at all.

My secondary schooling took me across town to a wonderful high school, Holy Names Academy, from 1961 to 1965. The years at Holy Names involved many shifting scenes in my kaleidoscope, most notably the civil rights movement and the Second Vatican Council of the Catholic Church. I can still remember the classroom where I was sitting when I first read Martin Luther King's "Letter from a Birmingham Jail" (1963). Idealistically, I thought that my generation might be the last to witness racial division and discrimination; I suspect my classmates "of color"—mostly Japanese, Filipina, and African-American—were less naive.

Our religion classes seemed to alternate between well-worn teachings—a dreadful monograph titled *Modern Youth and Chastity* and a manual of moral philosophy that debated the ethics of dueling are two artifacts of the time—and intimations of a church rethinking itself. We studied the 1963 encyclical of Pope John XXIII (1958–1963), *Pacem in Terris (Peace on Earth)*, the first papal encyclical to be addressed beyond Catholic borders to all "persons of goodwill." With its strong advocacy of human rights, call for disarmament, and discussion of the common good, this encyclical made a strong impression; in fact, it bears rereading today. Among the three characteristics of the modern age Pope John XXIII drew attention to was the "part that women are now playing in political life."

> This is a development that is perhaps of swifter growth among Christian nations, but it is also happening extensively, if more slowly, among nations that are heirs to different traditions and imbued with a differ-ent culture. Women are gaining an increasing aware-ness of their natural dignity. Far from being content with a purely passive role or allowing themselves to be regarded as a kind of instrument, they are demanding both in domestic and in public life the rights and duties which belong to them as human persons.[5]

The term *feminism* had not yet gained currency, but we were beginning to understand that women could do just about any-thing. Some of us inferred from *Pacem in Terris* that the Catholic Church might be an arena in which women's "rights and duties" could be exercised in new ways, but the recalci-trance of the hierarchical church has since chastened our hope.[6]

The burgeoning ecumenical movement provided impetus during my high school years to explore religious differences and to engage with those whose perspectives differed from my own. The opening of the Second Vatican Council on October 11, 1962, during my sophomore year, made it an exciting time to be a Catholic. Belonging to a church opening its windows to let in fresh air animated my interest in religion and provided a major motivation for my lifelong professional work in religious education. In my senior year (1965), a group of us sponsored an afternoon of conversation with the youth group from a nearby synagogue, Temple De Hirsch-Sinai. I also attended an ecumenical conference in which Robert McAfee Brown, a Presbyterian minister and well-known theologian who served as one of the official Protestant observers at Vatican II, gave the keynote address. Little did I imagine then that I would have the privilege of studying with him about a decade later at Union Theological Seminary in New York City or that I would one day be a guest speaker at Temple De Hirsch-Sinai.

Nor did I realize then that for the first time in history, the Catholic Church had formally recognized that other religions had a "ray of truth." In its Declaration on Non-Christian Religions (*Nostra Aetate*), the Second Vatican Council said:

> The Catholic Church rejects nothing that is true and holy in these religions. She regards with sincere reverence those ways of conduct and of life, those precepts and teachings which, though differing in many aspects from the ones she holds and sets forth, nonetheless often reflect a ray of that Truth which enlightens all men [and women].[7]

This declaration, of course, is the same one that initiated the revolution in relations between Catholics and Jews. Promulgated on October 28, 1965, about five months after my high school graduation, it took some time to become a part of my consciousness. I had other preoccupations.

A MARGINAL PLACE IN THE WORLD

My ecumenical and interreligious journey took a circuitous route, as I joined a women's religious community, the Sisters of the Holy Names of Jesus and Mary, in August 1965.[8] It was a calling without much drama—a sense of the abiding presence of God and a desire to follow a way of life that seemed to foster a generosity of heart and mind and spirit. My parents were not enthused, but they honored my desire to enter.

I spent the initial years of formation near Portland, Oregon, and then in Spokane, Washington, professing temporary vows on February 5, 1968, and final vows on June 17, 1972. My entry into the community just four months before the conclusion of Vatican II meant that our group experienced the turmoil of moving from a more confined understanding of religious life to that of the "nun in the modern world."[9] We chafed at many of the restrictions of our novitiate, though I never regretted the long periods of silence that were so much a part of our daily rhythm. We spent the second year of our novitiate under the tutelage of a wise novice director, who honored our questions and affectionately told us that she had never seen such a collection of strong-willed people gathered in one place!

The transition to be more fully "nuns in the world" was complicated. We debated passionately, even vociferously, among ourselves about what our appropriate role in the church and the world should be. We took with utmost seriousness one of the major mandates of Vatican II: the renewal of religious life.[10] Although our change in clothing from a full-length "habit" to "secular" clothes was the most visible one—and one of the most intensely argued, if settled long ago—our transformation lay primarily in educating ourselves to assume more responsibility for our lives and to lay claim to our distinctive vision as women of the church. We had inherited a largely monastic schedule ill-suited for the active life of educators, along with some traditions of spirituality inappropriate for women actively engaged beyond the confines of the "cloister." We embarked on the long and as yet unfinished project of fashioning a life together with a rhythm of prayer and work and leisure that sustained us as an "apostolic" community. This reclaiming of our own agency is one of the most important results of our renewal, and the modes of governance we have developed differ dramatically from the male models imposed in earlier years. I doubt I would have stayed in the community had we not experienced such a revitalizing of our life together.

As a congregation known historically for its commitment to education and to the arts, its members were then principally involved in the consuming work of running schools, with little opportunity for sustained interaction outside the Catholic realm.[11] Yet living in the religiously variegated and relatively "unchurched" Pacific Northwest meant we had more frequent contact with "non-Catholics" than would have been the case in places where Catholicism was dominant, such as the cities of the Eastern Seaboard.[12] We also interacted more with the religiously unaffiliated than would have been the case in places where Christianity suffused the culture, such as the South. The geographic location of my province also meant less awareness of the pervasive antisemitism than was characteristic of places such as Québec, where our congregation originated in 1843 and where many members still live.[13]

Religious life, as I have come to discover, offers distinct possibilities for engaging beyond the borders of one's denomination. By entering a community of women religious, I had seemingly set out on a "blue highway," a back road removed from society's major thoroughfares.[14] Indeed, as Sandra Schneiders observes, members of religious communities occupy a liminal position.[15] We have renounced marriage and the creation of a family, personal ownership and pursuit of corporate wealth, and full and independent participation in political life and processes. This marginality is not escapism but is intended to be prophetic: Religious life exists at the edge of society's system in order to recognize and repair how that system harms those it excludes. It is lived on the "thresholds where realities meet, clash, and merge."[16]

Yet the stereotypes persist of the nun as either the sweet naïf or harsh knuckle-rapper—and in any case, as asexual. I find such stereotypes infuriating. At times, I learn from them, as I did in a Catholic-Jewish conference in London in June 2000 that involved participants principally from the United Kingdom and the United States, a few European and Israeli scholars, and a delegation from the Vatican. Although the large number of participants hindered the flow of discussion, our exchange was for the most part candid and stimulating. Toward the latter part of the conference, one of the Catholics—a priest—launched into a lengthy, romantic, and sermonic discourse about Mary as virgin and mother. Its traditionalist theology and tangential relation to the point under discussion elicited considerable skepticism, if one might judge by the body language of rolled eyes and heads buried in hands. Many, including all the Catholic women, sought recognition by the chair to respond, but I have less recollection of the rejoinders than I do of the comment by the woman next to me. A Liberal rabbi from the U.K., she wrote furiously on her notepad: "Mary. Virgin. Why don't they talk about real women?"

That was a moment in which I experienced just how odd and anomalous religious life seems to many. While I suspect I understand what my table companion was objecting to, the starkness of her opposition of virgin and "real women" hit hard. In reflecting later, I realize I never use terminology about virginity to describe celibacy; not only does it connote a naive innocence, but it also speaks only to the dimension of abstention from genital sexual intimacy. Without question, this self-chosen abstention—or better, an abstention that is part of our being called to a distinctive way of life—has its ascetic aspects, though I often feel that whatever asceticism it demands pales beside that required of mothers. Nevertheless, the term *virginity* seems to suggest that we have repressed our sexuality, thereby ceasing to be "real" women. It gives little hint of the inner autonomy celibacy can offer. Celibacy does not eradicate one's sexuality, and the deep friendships that community fosters nourish one's affective life.

Consecrated celibacy, however, is completely uncharacteristic of rabbinic Judaism, which places intense emphasis on family life and home-based ritual.[17] So to be with Jews as a member of a religious congregation is to experience our liminality—our oddness—on a regular basis. While at times this awareness can be jarring, as it was at that conference, in general it has increased my sensitivity to the peculiarities of religious life, a sensitivity that can be dulled by remaining in the more homogeneous company of one's religious congregation. At the same time, it makes the God question more prominent. Jews typically are more reticent in speaking about God, a healthy corrective to the overfamiliarity with which many Christians tend to speak about the Holy One.[18] The presence, however, of persons for whom the "God quest" is the principal explanation for a liminal way of life puts the Divine-human relationship, at least implicitly, on the agenda of Jewish-Christian dialogue.

TEACHING

During this tumultuous time in the culture, church, and community, I began my teaching career at the secondary level at Holy Names Academy in Spokane, after graduating from Fort Wright College in 1969 with a double major in religion and the humanities. Fortunate to have had a wonderful "master" teacher to mentor me, I reveled in the interaction and learning the classroom provided. It was all-consuming, with classes and extracurricular activities: sports, retreats, student council, and debate. Certified by the State of Washington as a teacher of English, I also taught a number of religion classes. They quickly became my first love—and a great challenge. We were committed to making religion "relevant," which is no small challenge with adolescents in any era, but was particularly daunting in the wake of Vatican II. I confess I tried my fair share of "finding Christ" in films and literature, and likely oversaw the creation of more collages than was educationally and theologically prudent. Nevertheless, we all worked very hard to provide an intellectually and spiritually substantive religion curriculum. And I like to think that on many days we succeeded.

During this period when "renewal" of religious life was a watchword among us, I discovered Abraham Joshua Heschel's work, initially his book on the prophets. His book contributed significantly to my love not only of the prophetic writings but also of the "Old" Testament, as I then called it.[19] It is a book to which I return regularly, particularly to reflect on his profound insight into God's pathos, which has been so formative for my understanding of God.[20] I also engaged in some modest ecumenical activity with local evangelical churches. Those were the early days of the Catholic charismatic movement—Pentecostalism in liturgical dress—and I participated in a number of prayer meetings, only to grow disillusioned by the anti-intellectualism I experienced.

My five years of teaching at the secondary level significantly shaped me. I became a student of the educational process as well as the Bible (I aspired at the time to study for a doctorate in New Testament), and this dual commitment decisively shaped not only my graduate studies but also my entire professional life. Teaching is the most significant way in which I learn, both from the study involved in preparing for classes and from the interaction that happens with students and other faculty members.

Thanks to the willingness of our province's leadership team to send me to New York City for graduate school, in the fall of

1974 I entered the doctoral program in religion and education jointly sponsored by Union Theological Seminary and Teachers College, Columbia University. These schools stand across Broadway from one another, and also across from the Jewish Theological Seminary of America, where Abraham Joshua Heschel had taught before his death in 1972. As I walked the streets of my new Morningside Heights neighborhood—the "Academic Acropolis," as one map calls it—I regretted that I had never had the opportunity to learn in the presence of Rabbi Heschel. Only years later would I meet his wife, Sylvia, an accomplished pianist, and come to know his daughter Susannah, a scholar whose expertise in modern German Protestant thought makes a major contribution to Jewish-Christian relations. Although my forays into the Jewish Theological Seminary were few—I felt very much a stranger then—my studies in Christian origins and biblical hermeneutics at Union opened up a new world of thinking about the relationship between Judaism and Christianity.

I began to grapple with the complexity of the church's emergence from formative Judaism, and I realized how simplistically we had learned and taught this development. I realized with increasing dismay the chasm between the findings of biblical scholars and theologians and what preachers and teachers were saying. In particular, I became more critical of the motif of "salvation history," which we had used in introducing our students to the Bible in those high school religion classes. It became the subject of my doctoral dissertation and my first sustained theological contribution to the conversation between Judaism and Christianity.[21] Most of those theological conversations at that juncture, however, were with other Christians, most notably with my mentor, Fr. Raymond E. Brown. His enormous erudition, eagerness to learn from Jewish scholars, dedication to scholarship in the service of the church, support for women, and great kindness exercised a profound influence on me. His sudden death at age seventy in August 1998 was a tremendous loss, not only for his colleagues, students, and friends, but also for the church and for relations between Christians and Jews.

Yet, if in those days I learned theology principally from Christians, a few Jewish classmates from Teachers College became my instructors in Jewish life. Intense conversations after classes, supplemented by exposure to New York's Jewish culture, expanded my education. A classmate with whom I remain in touch invited me to her family's Seder in Dayton, Ohio. It was my first Seder, and I was the only non-Jew amid her large extended family, but the hospitality they extended enabled me to feel comfortable.

Meanwhile, Boston had become home to me. I began teaching at Boston College in the fall of 1977. Sara's native city is justly famous for its labyrinthine streets and gridlock, but it opened up new horizons in the interreligious realm. Invited to join the Catholic-Jewish Committee, which met monthly to discuss an array of issues, I became part of a network of men and women from various walks of life who cared deeply about the relationship between our two communities. I made my first trip to Israel in the late 1970s with a group of Jews and Catholics from the Boston area led by longtime members and friends Rabbi Murray Rothman (a part-time colleague in the Boston College theology department) and Father Robert Bullock, a local pastor active in Jewish-Catholic relations. The scholarship of colleagues at Boston College, particularly that of Anthony J. Saldarini and Donald Dietrich, furthered my knowledge of Judaica and of the Holocaust.[22] Sadly, Rabbi Rothman, Fr. Bullock, and Professor Saldarini have died; I am grateful for the riches they shared with me.

I wrote my first article on the implications of Jewish-Christian dialogue in the early 1980s, "Questions Which 'Touch on the Heart of Faith.'"[23] I remember how important the essay became to me as I was working on it, but I had no sense of how the questions I took up then would persist and intensify. A sabbatical in 1983 gave me the privilege of spending a semester at the Ecumenical Institute for Theological Research at Tantur, on Jerusalem's southern boundary. Living in Israel allowed me to experience being a member of a minority religion, and it revealed the tortuous complexity of the Arab-Israeli relationship and the politics of the Middle East. It also exposed me to diverse Christianities (e.g., Arabic-speaking Greek Orthodox, Copts, Armenians), gave entree into various groups of Jews and Christians engaged in dialogue (e.g., The Rainbow Group in Jerusalem), and provided occasion for contact with the Sisters of Sion, who have become increasingly important to me because of their communal commitment to the Jewish people.[24] My experience during that sabbatical, reinforced by many subsequent trips, has given me a feel for the importance of the Land of Israel in Jewish life. Above all, Israel itself became tangible—a tiny nation-state in which two peoples struggle to live together—not simply the rarefied "Holy Land." I feel obliged to "pray for the peace of Jerusalem."[25]

THE ECUMENICAL
AND INTERRELIGIOUS CHALLENGE

After returning from Israel, I devoted attention to acquiring more extensive knowledge about Christianity's relationship with Judaism. As a religious and theological educator seeking to understand, practice, and teach about the Christian life, it became imperative to probe not merely our roots in Judaism but also our long and difficult relationship over the centuries.[26] In addition to drawing upon the scholarly resources of the academic realm, I was fortunate to be a part of a group of Catholics and Jews in the Boston area who met monthly to discuss a range of issues.

Then, in 1985, I met Sara Lee. Our friendship and collaborative projects opened up new realms of learning. A few years later I was invited to join the Christian Scholars Group on Christian-Jewish Relations (CSG); membership in this ecumenical study group, which meets twice a year to discuss papers from scholars both within and beyond our group, has been an invaluable source of knowledge, and the collegial relations our group enjoys are a model of academic discourse.[27]

Over the years I have made my own the conviction of my CSG colleague Clark Williamson that "conversation with Jews is indispensable to understanding the Christian faith." History testifies that "apart from listening to and talking with Jews, we will misunderstand the Christian faith and act on our misunderstandings."[28] The intensity with which I hold this conviction has energized many of my writings since the mid-1980s, yet it appears to have had relatively little effect on colleagues in the field of religious education. With a few exceptions, they do not seem to recognize how foundational "conversation with Jews" is to the education of Christians.[29]

Increasingly in the past decade or so, more of my energies have been devoted to Jewish-Christian relations. More than once I've quipped that if I had known I would have become so involved in this realm, I would have gotten a "proper education" beyond my two years of biblical Hebrew: the study of modern Hebrew, the Talmud, and Jewish liturgical life. These regrets aside, however, I think I learned a "feel" for Judaism through friendships that no amount of scholarship can replace. I continue to learn from Jewish colleagues and sources, as well as from Christians learned in aspects of Judaism.

Little did I realize when I began teaching how profoundly ecumenical and interreligious dialogue would affect my life, both personally and professionally. After seventeen years on the faculty of Boston College, a large Catholic university, in 1994 I returned to Union Theological Seminary, a historically

Protestant and now ecumenical graduate school remarkable
for its diverse racial, ethnic, and denominational mix.
Ecumenical dialogue is an implicit part of the daily work,
whether in classes or in the myriad activities beyond the classroom. Because students in any given class range from Seventh-
day Adventist to Unitarian-Universalist—and everything in
between those denominational extremes—teaching at Union is
a daily challenge in expanding religious horizons and fostering
ways of learning from differences.[30]

The ecumenical challenge is also deeply personal. It is not
easy to be a Catholic at Union. Some students come with
deeply ingrained misconceptions, such as believing we worship
Mary, idolize statues, and have no knowledge of the Bible.
Others, raised as Catholics, have left Catholic life for other
denominations, often because they experienced the church as
rigid ("I couldn't breathe in the Catholic Church," a recently
ordained Presbyterian pastor told me) or as inhospitable (particularly to gays and lesbians). Some who have left Catholicism
have scars from encounters with insensitive officials, and their
anger, while understandable, complicates ecumenical dialogue.
And then there are the very real problems of Catholic life, such
as the second-class status of women, its tendency toward
authoritarianism, and the sexual abuse crisis. I found it excru-
ciating to be at Union during the height of that crisis, which
revealed so many troubled clergy and so few wise bishops. Yet
my years at Union have also deepened my appreciation for the
depth and breadth of the Catholic tradition, even as they have
enabled me to work ecumenically. Union is a place where I
work to use my own textured particularism to contribute to
religious pluralism.

Hailing as I do from Seattle, which has been called the
"nation's Upper West Side," it seems fitting that I like living in
my "'hood," the Upper West Side of Manhattan. In particular,
I am grateful for Union's location across the street from the

Jewish Theological Seminary of America, one of two seminaries in the United States for the Conservative Movement of Judaism. Over the years I have come to work with its colleagues and students primarily through its William Davidson School of Jewish Education. At times I have taught courses with Professor Carol Ingall of the Davidson faculty, and a number of JTS students have taken courses at Union with me and with other Union faculty. All of this heightens my belief that the educational process is a necessary component of Jewish-Christian dialogue.[31]

Yet leading such processes involves far more than skills. It depends upon practicing what Nicholas Burbules has called the "communicative virtues," general dispositions and practices that help support successful communicative relations with a variety of people over time. They include tolerance, patience, an openness to give and receive criticism, a readiness to admit that one may be mistaken, the desire to reinterpret or translate one's own concerns so that they will be comprehensible to others, the self-imposition of restraint in order that others may speak, and the willingness to listen thoughtfully and attentively.[32] Dialogue, then, is not only an outcome of a careful educational process but also a way of life that requires a great deal of work, including constant control of ego needs. I find it a deeply religious activity. I consider it a privilege to teach Christians and Jews, and occasionally some Muslims, Buddhists, and Hindus, in the presence of the other. Although I did not set out to work in an ecumenical and interreligious context, I consider it one of the great graces of my life.

REVISING CHRISTIAN THEOLOGY:
A SACRED OBLIGATION

In my experience, interreligious dialogue is a manifestation of God's graciousness in our time, when we are called to learn to be "religious interreligiously."[33] In response, we are called to engage in the lifelong task of rethinking Christian self-understanding. This demand is all the more compelling in relation to Judaism because so much of how we think about Christianity has been built upon a distorted portrait of Judaism. This daunting task, which I began in my book, *Has God Only One Blessing? Judaism as a Source of Christian Self-Understanding*, is at once the great challenge and vital gift of relationships with knowledgeable Jews. It is also, as our Christian Scholars Group expresses it, a "sacred obligation":

> We believe that revising Christian teaching about Judaism and the Jewish people is a central and indispensable obligation of theology in our time. It is essential that Christianity both understand and represent Judaism accurately, not only as a matter of justice for the Jewish people, but also for the integrity of Christian faith, which we cannot proclaim without reference to Judaism.[34]

My own encounter with living Jewish tradition inspires a passion to develop ways of educating in faith that foster religious commitments that are clear and rooted—grounding persons in the tradition's way of life—yet simultaneously ambiguous and adaptive, recognizing the inadequacy of any one expression of faith in face of the infinite God. It compels me to develop more adequate ways of interpreting scripture, celebrating liturgy, and drawing upon our symbol systems.[35]

Reconstructing one's theology may *seem* like a cerebral task—and, without question, it *is* intellectually demanding—but it is also a deeply emotional process. My visceral sense of the finitude of Christianity has deepened as my knowledge of Jewish-Christian relations has developed. If we are to heal the "still open wounds" of history and ameliorate the "teaching of contempt," we must probe the ways in which Christian theology legitimized the disparagement of Judaism and vilification of Jews.[36] Facing this reality is a humbling task because it involves taking on the shame of our history. For example, several years ago I spoke to a group of Holocaust survivors in tandem with the author of a novel about the impact of the Spanish Inquisition on Jews.[37] Yes, I could at least partially explain the factors that shaped the church's mentality of sixteenth-century Spain. But *this* audience knew far better than I that the prejudices and persecution of the late medieval church provided fertile ground on which "the venomous plant of hatred for the Jews was to flourish" in *their* lives.[38] As one member of the audience asked me after another lecture, "How could those who believed in the Gospel of Jesus Christ have done such atrocities in his name?" For such questions our catechisms provide no answers.

Although the Christian churches, and the Catholic Church in particular, have recently expressed sorrow and repentance for past sins against the Jews, and resolved that the "spoiled seeds of anti-Judaism and antisemitism must never again be allowed to take root in any human heart," such expressions do not yet sufficiently permeate Christian self-understanding.[39] Catholics have some excellent documents about our relationship with the Jewish people and tradition, but too frequently the insights of those documents remain isolated from other doctrinal statements.

I experienced this chasm between official documents and everyday life in the church during the controversy in 2002–2003 over Mel Gibson's film, *The Passion of the Christ*. Having a long interest in the interpretation of the Gospel narratives of the passion and death of Jesus dating back to my days as a graduate student of Raymond Brown, author of a monumental, two-volume work, *The Death of Jesus*, I was among the team of Catholic and Jewish scholars who reviewed a script of the film and sent a lengthy memorandum to the

Gibson team about our concerns. After I viewed the film when it opened on February 25, 2004 (Ash Wednesday), my distress deepened. As I saw it, Gibson had portrayed Jews as implacable enemies of Jesus who demanded his brutal death, which the Roman-appointed governor of Judea, Pontius Pilate, reluctantly agreed to only to mollify the bloodthirsty Jewish mob. Gibson added many scenes with no basis in the Gospels; these scenes depicted the Jews, most especially Caiaphas and the Sanhedrin, as malevolent, sadistic, and satanic. The film reverses entirely the power dynamic between the Roman Empire and the Jewish people, and thereby falsifies history.[40]

Were Gibson to have claimed he was simply exercising his artistic license, I would feel different. What is problematic is his assertion that his film is the most reliable account of the passion ever produced and his assumption of the high moral ground. He wrapped himself in the mantle of one form of Catholic piety while in fact not in full communion with the church. He expressed contempt for the teachings of Vatican II and then accused us of persecuting him, claiming that scholars (presumably our team) perverted the Gospel.

Had this been simply a clash between a filmmaker's vision and the sensibility of scholars, the controversy would not have been so distressing, especially because we learned early on how masterfully this celebrity used us to garner and sustain publicity. What was—and remains—far more painful is what this controversy revealed about the state of dialogue in the church itself. Those of us who raised questions about the film were attacked as "dupes of the Jews," "forces of Satan," the "arrogant gang of so-called scholars," and even as "antichrists." "You have mail" took on a new meaning, as hateful messages filled our electronic mail. We reported at length to a leading Catholic authority about these attacks; he listened to us, but offered neither a pastoral word of support nor a public defense. It will be a long time before I get over this act of betrayal.

Although I have been aware for some time that there are many angry people in the world for whom the vocabulary of religion provides fodder for the expression of hate, the controversy over the film exposed serious rifts within the church. It is not the difference of opinion that bothers me, but the absolute lack of Christian charity—and the general failure of our leaders to address this. The controversy also revealed how little the general Catholic public and even many of the clergy know about church teaching of the past forty years about Jews and Judaism. In particular, I learned how little most Catholics know about interpreting our Gospels in their historical and literary contexts. Catholicism has developed a substantive and impressive body of literature on biblical interpretation, much of it relevant to dialogue with Jews. Although I do not work primarily as a biblical scholar, it is important for me to help make this body of interpretation more widely accessible in the church, as an important way of helping persons understand changes in the church's posture toward Jews.[41]

THE GRACE OF INTERRELIGIOUS ENCOUNTER

Interreligious encounter reveals the incomprehensibility of God, who alone is infinite and absolute. God's spaciousness exposes the limited perspectives of one's own religious tradition. Even as I believe ardently in the Way of Christianity and aspire to live it as a practicing Roman Catholic, I know it does not exhaust the paths by which God draws us—and I cannot believe it is *the* superior way by which God calls *all* to walk. In the theological realm, this means reexamining the traditional affirmations of Christianity regarding Jesus as Lord and Savior of all in light of the knowledge and wisdom gained through interreligious encounter. Traditional doctrinal formulations are important; they express the continuity of faith over the ages, and they should not be swept aside in mere fervor for what is new. Neither, however, should they become idols. The church articulated them in particular times and cultures in response to specific crises; they must be interpreted in their historical context. It is the church's task to discern the Spirit's movement in every age.

Surely we must detect the movement of the Spirit in the dissolution of walls of misunderstanding, intolerance, and enmity among religious groups. When women and men of deep, if differing, faiths come together in our time to share across the boundaries of their traditions, is it not the Spirit at work, inspiring us to conceptualize our relationship with other religions in terms that our ancestors in faith could not have imagined? Those who speak in the name of the church must listen attentively to those at the forefront of interreligious dialogue who have spent years pondering its meaning.

Over the years I have come to envy the emphasis on study and learning in Judaism. Although Catholicism, too, has a long tradition of respect for the life of the mind, many of its authorities seem ambivalent about critical thinking in the theological realm. In the schools where I have taught, I have always experienced freedom to pursue thinking, wherever it led. In the contemporary church, however, too many leaders show disinterest in learning or, in some cases, disdain for thought that stretches beyond their own boundaries. "Is it a healthy state of affairs," journalist Peter Steinfels asks, "when leading church officials perceive those trained to explicate the faith as, in fact, prime threats to it?"[42]

As I worked on this chapter, I read Vanessa Ochs's memoir of her year in Jerusalem seeking a deeper connection to Judaism without sacrificing her feminist convictions.[43] Her book is filled with references to the importance of Torah study, from which women have largely been excluded until recently and remain so in many Orthodox communities. The way in which generations of male authorities have regarded women as a threat to "true Torah" has its analogies with the distrust many Catholic hierarchs show toward theologians, especially women committed to feminist theology. Yet, in many of the Jewish communities of my acquaintance, the passion for learning is much more widespread and palpable than it is in similar Catholic settings. My wish is that this passion would permeate our church more deeply and broadly.

In my experience, dialogue with Jews deepens appreciation for mystery, for the ungraspable nature of truth, for the "more than" of religious experience. It has stimulated me to ponder more profoundly the One Beyond All Names and to probe more seriously who this God is who "saves" and "redeems." It has challenged me to wrestle with painful questions of God's absence or powerlessness that arise out of reflection on the Shoah. Thus, I find that Judaism, particularly as Jewish friends and colleagues mediate it, reveals new layers of meaning in my vocation insofar as it opens up new—if often unsettling—vistas on God.

At the same time, my immersion in a woman's religious congregation provides a sort of compass for walking along the interreligious road. Engagement with the religious other has intensified my desire to be a learned, committed Catholic. It may be that my location in a community—albeit one with few involvements with Jews and Judaism—contributes to this. Sandra Schneiders suggests that because members of religious communities are absorbed in the God-quest as the primary concern of their lives, they are "sensitively attuned to religious and spiritual developments inside and outside the church." Belonging to a religious order allows one to be "at once very deeply involved in institutional Catholicism and often widely and deeply involved in the experiences of spirituality beyond its denominational boundaries."[44] Religious life provides me an atmosphere in which permeable boundaries can be developed and maintained.

In subsequent chapters, Sara and I will discuss the nature of our work together. It is through this partnership in teaching that we have been privileged to take one another into our religious worlds and thereby gain another perspective on our own.

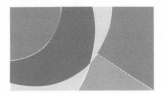

4

INTERRELIGIOUS TEACHING
AND LEARNING:
THE EXPERIENCE

"Christian-Jewish dialogue" appears at first glance to convey a simple, yet important, message. Given the history of their relationships, and events such as the Shoah and Vatican II, Christians and Jews need to learn more about each other and develop insights that will heal the rifts that have divided them. Yet the phrase covers a range of possibilities. Our experience is that when Christians and Jews engage in dialogue *in the presence of the other*, the conversation is deeper and more transformative. This experience is at the heart of our collaboration.

In this chapter, we will describe our most significant projects in the hope of giving the reader insight into interreligious learning and the transformative effect of studying in the presence of the religious other. In this way, we will illumine our distinct perspective on dialogue between Christians and Jews.

Our major projects have focused on Catholics and Jews (although not exclusively). This is not to mitigate the importance of Jews interacting with Protestant and Orthodox Christians as well. Rather, it reflects our own commitments as a Jew and a Catholic and the distinctive relationship between the Catholic Church and the Jewish people over the course of nearly two thousand years.[1]

In this chapter, we describe five projects:

- The Catholic-Jewish Colloquium: An Experiment in Interreligious Learning

- Educating for Religious Particularism and Pluralism

- Consultation on Teacher Preparation for Educating for Religious Particularism and Pluralism

- Interreligious Learning Workshops for Teachers

- Consultation at the Hong Kong International School

We have sought to describe the foci and activities of these projects in a way that will provide a sense of what we did and what we believe participants learned. In chapter 5, we will discuss the educational thinking that underlies our projects.

THE CATHOLIC-JEWISH COLLOQUIUM: AN EXPERIMENT IN INTERRELIGIOUS LEARNING

Our journey together as guides to interreligious learning began with few road maps. Over the course of collaborating on papers for the Association of Professors and Researchers in Religious Education (APRRE) and our mutual interest in building bridges between our two traditions through education, we developed some preliminary ideas about bringing together Catholic and Jewish educators. Yet we set out on our initial project, the Catholic-Jewish Colloquium, without knowing precisely how to proceed. It grew organically, as each session in turn suggested the next. As our longest project—nearly three years—it has served as the foundation for our continuing work. Through our work on the Colloquium, we identified important principles about interreligious learning, but these principles emerged in the process of our retrospective analysis, especially in writing together about the experience in a special issue of *Religious Education*, for which we served as guest editors.[2]

Although neither of us had much experience in leading interreligious dialogue, we shared a particular point of view as educators. A passion for the work of religious education, common principles about teaching and learning, insights into religious formation, and a sensitivity to principles about adult learning shaped our thinking as we set about creating this experiment. We decided to center our project on religious educators from our two faith communities because we believed that they have a singular contribution to make in the formation of religious identity. Religious education within one's faith tradition not only provides the foundation for self-understanding as a member of that tradition, but it also shapes attitudes, either negative or positive, about religious others. How teachers interpret the fundamental narratives of Judaism and Christianity not only tells learners who they are but also has, in many cases, resulted in a negative or reductionist portrayal of the other. Without providing historical context and an understanding of how Judaism and Christianity have related over the centuries, religious educators may inadvertently convey distorted views that hinder mutual understanding. We spent hours discussing such matters as we explored possible foci.

We decided to seek a grant from the Lilly Endowment in Indianapolis, Indiana, and our meeting in 1991 with program officer Dr. James Wind proved an important turning point. When we arrived at the Lilly offices, we thought the important task was to immerse Catholic educators in the post–Vatican II understandings of the relationship between Judaism and their own tradition. We also thought it was vital for them to encounter Judaism as a living, vibrant tradition in its own right through contact with knowledgeable, serious Jews. Dr. Wind challenged our assumption that Jews should be witnesses rather than full partners in this effort. Was there not, he asked, some changed perspective significant for Jewish educators? By the time we reached the Indianapolis airport to head back to our respective homes, we had already begun reworking our proposal in a way that established Jewish and Catholic educators as equal partners in learning together.

We hoped that both Jewish and Catholic participants would undergo changed perspectives of the other. Yet the specific transformative effect would differ. We anticipated challenging the Catholics to reconstruct their theological self-understanding in light of Vatican II and subsequent teachings on relations with Judaism. We desired to help Jewish participants understand the changes in church teaching that placed Catholics in a posture that differed dramatically from previous centuries.

Our previous experience led us to assume that the Catholic participants would be shaped by the prevalent view of Christianity as superseding Judaism: Jesus Christ and the life of the church had made Judaism obsolete. We anticipated that supersessionism would be most familiar to the Catholics in terms of understanding the relationship between the Testaments, with the "Old" Testament regarded as a promise and the New Testament as its fulfillment. One of our goals was to provide resources that would give them a more nuanced understanding of the relationship between the Testaments and a more in-depth knowledge of the emergence of Christianity from Judaism.

Jews, we had reason to assume, would come with attitudes toward Christianity formed by their knowledge of history. The centuries of persecution of Jews in lands where Christianity exercised power meant that most Jews viewed Christians as responsible for their victimization. Even in the face of the church's changes in attitude and behavior, Jews, operating on feelings of mistrust, did not really know how to respond. So we decided we needed to make accessible contemporary church teachings, including recent Catholic studies that dealt frankly with Catholics' largely tragic relationship with Jews.

We believed that transformation was more likely to happen in people who were *studying in the presence of the other.* Accordingly, we designed the Colloquium to facilitate encounter with *the tradition as embodied in the other.* We wanted to transcend learning *about* the other in the abstract. Our interest lay primarily in providing ways in which participants might meet Judaism or Catholicism as *it was lived by informed, committed Jewish and Catholic educators.*[3]

Although we held strong convictions about the transformative challenges of our two groups of participants, we realized that accomplishing them would be messy. We anticipated that participants would experience cognitive disequilibrium as previously held beliefs, perceptions, and stereotypes were challenged. We assumed that participants would at times feel intimidated when confronted by questions about their own faith tradition that they felt unable to answer adequately. Nevertheless, we resolved to create an educational process that would be rigorous, yet sensitive to the concerns participants would bring to the Colloquium.

Given our goals and funds, we decided to limit the number of participants so that we could have a series of meetings and work in depth. Having advertised in selected national journals, we chose eleven educators from each tradition. We decided to hold our meetings in a neutral space in order to enhance the comfort level of the participants, and so we selected a conference center in Baltimore, near the Institute for Christian-Jewish Studies, which administered our grant money.[4] To prepare for our first session in February 1993, we spent a year studying and planning together, meeting whenever our schedules allowed, as well as by phone.

We convened six sessions of the Colloquium over the course of nearly six years:

SESSION I   *February 21–23, 1993*

Exploring Differences as a Means of Establishing
Common Ground: The Asymmetrical Character of
Judaism and Christianity

> Participants focused on scripture as a common
> source and as source of division. We led them in an
> analogy exercise about the relationship between the
> Tanakh (the Jewish Bible) and the New Testament.
> The differences between Catholic examples and
> Jewish examples illuminated the problems related to
> the assumptions of a shared scripture. A text study of
> Genesis 22 (the "binding" or "sacrifice" of Isaac) using
> Christian and Jewish commentaries illustrated the
> different interpretive lenses that each tradition brings
> to the same text.

SESSION II   *June 22–23, 1993*

Jews and Christians in the First Two Centuries

> Participants analyzed the protracted, complex, and
> polemical separation between Judaism and
> Christianity in the first two centuries. Participants
> came prepared to discuss questions we had sent
> ahead in connection with the two books they had
> been assigned.[5] Guest scholar Anthony J. Saldarini led
> a study of two Jewish reform movements illustrated
> by the Gospel of Matthew and the Dead Sea Scrolls.[6]
> He extended discussion into the late second century
> to show common moves to consolidate, legitimize,
> and institutionalize interpretations (e.g., *Mekilta de
> Rabbi Ishmael*, Epistle of Barnabas, *Didache*, and
> *Mishnah Berakot*).

SESSION III   *October 31–November 1, 1993*

Revisiting History in the Presence of the Other

> Participants focused on the High Middle Ages and
> Enlightenment and their impact on both Christianity
> and Judaism. In preparation, participants read two
> books on the history of the Jewish-Christian relation-
> ship.[7] Guest scholar Michael Signer led text studies on
> Anselm, Nahmanides, Gregory IX, and Rashi; he

lectured on the Enlightenment and Romanticism.[8] He also led a discussion on contemporary Jewish-Christian relations, using selected church documents.

SESSION IV   *January 9–10, 1994*

Judaism and Catholicism in the North American Context

Guest scholars John Coleman and Hasia Diner focused on the formative role of the immigrant experience, the interaction between communities of faith and North American culture, and the sociological and historical perspectives on interreligious learning.[9] Boys and Lee shared reflections on their visit to the United States Holocaust Memorial Museum in Washington, D.C., as a way of initiating dialogue about the Shoah.

SESSION V   *May 1–3, 1994*

The Educational Tasks of Catholic-Jewish Dialogue

Participants designed projects for interreligious learning. Guest scholar Celia Deutsch led a text study of Matthew 17:1–8. Participants engaged in peer teaching on texts and spirituality. Panelists Deutsch, Don Goor, and Elizabeth Losinski reflected on the story of their involvement in Catholic-Jewish dialogue.[10]

SESSION VI   *November 12–13, 1995*

Religious Educators and the Work of Interreligious Learning

Participants turned their attention to the relationship between particularism and pluralism and the task of integrating the Colloquium into their educational work. Boys and Lee used a contemporary icon ("Mary the 'Captive Daughter of Zion'" by Robert Lentz) as a case in point to illustrate the complexity of our respective symbol systems. Participants shared a practice, text, or belief from their tradition that they understood differently because of the Colloquium. A final session examined the relationship between the Colloquium and the fundamental tasks of religious education, with help from visiting scholar Dorothy C. Bass.[11]

In the richness of the exchanges among participants, the range of emotions and comments revealed how deeply the experience touched the core of what they believed as Catholics and Jews, as well as what they perceived about the other. Certain topics generated both new understandings and new discomforts. Revisiting the first and second century was the beginning of a journey of discovery for many Catholic participants:

> It struck me—almost as a bolt out of the blue—that this experience of the Colloquium promises (threatens?) to be life-changing. As I look at the roots of what I have believed and professed for all of my life, there are some very problematic areas which emerge.[12]

For Jews, exploring how Jesus and his followers fit into the pattern of Jewish sectarianism of the time moved them beyond a simplistic understanding of how Judaism and Christianity eventually parted ways. One Jewish participant remarked that given the existence of these Jewish groups, he was not sure what choices he would have made as a Jew living at that time. In listening to how Catholic participants talked about Jesus, another Jewish participant said:

> Listening to several insights about Jesus was especially memorable. Though I had thought about Jesus as a historical figure ... I had never been able to relate to or really understand the spirituality of Jesus. In fact, it was something I felt quite uncomfortable with. Listening to my new colleagues that day brought an "aha" of both understanding and appreciation, which was both exhilarating and scary.[13]

Given the long shadow that the Shoah casts over both Jewish history and relations between Christians and Jews, we were uncertain about how prominent a role it should play in our deliberations. We considered organizing a field trip for participants to the United States Holocaust Memorial Museum in Washington, D.C., not far from our Baltimore conference center. In the end, however, we decided against this, thinking that the Holocaust might come to dominate the whole Colloquium, reinforcing in Jewish participants a sense of themselves as victims and paralyzing the Catholic participants with shame. Instead, several months before Session IV, we spent a day together at the museum, which we found terribly moving and emotionally draining. We then talked well into the evening about what we had experienced and how we might best share that with participants.

We chose to limit explicit discussion of the Holocaust to an evening session, using reflections based on our time at the museum as a point of departure. We posed two questions, first asking the Jewish participants: "Given the centrality of the Holocaust to contemporary Jewish identity, what do you want to convey to Catholics that might help them gain new insights about its significance?" Then we asked the entire group: "What does all this [the Holocaust, its impact on Jewish identity, the complicity of Christians, and the church's recent attempts to confront this history] mean in terms of conversation between Catholics and Jews?" These questions, however, did not initiate the sort of discussion we had anticipated; the conversation was diffuse and somewhat tense. In retrospect, we should not have been surprised that even a group of Jews and Catholics who had grown to trust and care for one another over eleven months would find it difficult to discuss the Shoah.

Perhaps we might also read the difficulty of this conversation as an indication of the sensitivity our participants manifested toward one another. As the sessions of the Colloquium continued, we were deeply moved by what we witnessed. The participants had taken on new understandings of, and attitudes toward, the practices and beliefs of the other tradition, and they had expanded the horizons of their own religious identity. This must be seen against the backdrop of a well-documented history of conflict leading to Jewish mistrust of Christians and Christian feelings of ambivalence and guilt.

The participants themselves articulate this more powerfully than we can. For example, in response to studying both the Tanakh (the Jewish Bible) and the New Testament, a Jewish participant shared the following:

> My second memory comes from the first Colloquium: Jews and Catholics studying the scriptures. When I study Torah, I recite a blessing over the study of God's word. As we studied the Christian scriptures, I felt a need to say a blessing as well. The traditional blessing would have been inappropriate. But I felt sad that I had no blessing to say.[14]

This comment underscores the complexity of the two traditions sharing major portions of the same scripture, yet interpreting it differently, while also learning to interpret Christian sacred texts in their historical context.[15]

With new insights about history, both groups developed changed understandings about themselves and the religious other. One Jewish participant, reacting to the challenge of Jewish self-understanding based on victimization at the hands of Christians, observed the following:

> When we say Jews read history as victims, we are still coming from the perspective that we are victims and that Christians are potential perpetrators…. If I view myself, a Jew, as a victim, then I actually practice Judaism differently. It takes on the role of a weight that I have to try and get out from under, so that I can

become someone who is free from the slings and
arrows of outrageous misfortune.[16]

In both groups, the problems of how the history of their religions is taught was an enduring question. For the Catholics, it
was often a matter of what had been omitted that led to a perception of Judaism as principally a biblical religion without
any understanding of the ongoing history and evolution of
Judaism, to say nothing of its interaction with Christians and
Christianity through the ages. One Catholic participant
summed up the dilemma:

> I'd like to say in terms of our history with the Jews …
> I think by and large if we were honest what we
> would say is that in terms of our programs, after
> Jesus died and we [teachers] spent a little time with
> Paul and the Acts, we just ignore them [Jews].… It's
> like in our post–New Testament the Jews just van-
> ished from the face of the earth in terms of our con-
> sciousness.[17]

Looking back, we are conscious that the nearly three years of
our work with the Catholic-Jewish Colloquium were
immensely influential for our subsequent collaboration. We
have a clear sense that the participants embarked on a significant journey, both in terms of understanding the religious other
as well as their own tradition. Without question, important
issues remained unresolved. Interreligious learning leads to
broader and deeper questions. What was palpable was a sense
of excitement at what we had achieved together, new bonds of
friendship and loyalty based on our learning together, and a
deeper understanding and appreciation of the profundity of the
process of interreligious learning. We also came to understand
how difficult it is to engage in the work of transformation,

both individually and as members of religious traditions. As one participant said:

> And to stop seeing ourselves and the other in those ways is to really start out on a journey that has no script and that is really frightening. On some basic level you understand it is re-crafting a whole sense of self. And perhaps re-crafting a sense of self in relationship to the other in ways that you do not know is ...[18]

The fact that this participant's comment trails off rather than reaches a conclusion symbolizes the Colloquium experience. It was a point of departure, not the achievement of a destination.

As the creators and leaders of the Colloquium, we emerged with strengthened convictions and new insights and questions that inspired us to find new opportunities for interreligious teaching and learning in a variety of venues. Writing about the Colloquium for the issue of *Religious Education* gave rise to initial musings about the role religious commitments might play in fostering religious pluralism. Those musings, in turn, motivated us to pursue a new grant.

EDUCATING FOR RELIGIOUS PARTICULARISM AND PLURALISM

In 1997 we met to formulate a grant proposal in the hope of addressing questions that had grown out of the Colloquium:

- What sort of education and formation in faith enable persons to participate intelligently in a religiously pluralistic society?

- What sort of education provides persons of faith with the grounding to engage in religious questions with people of other faith?

- What sort of education prepares persons to draw upon
  their commitment of faith in the public square in order
  to foster the common good?

With the encouragement of our friend and colleague Dorothy
Bass, who had been a visiting scholar at the final session of the
Colloquium, we applied to the project she directs, the
Valparaiso Project on the Education and Formation of People
in Faith. It seemed a natural home for the kind of exploration
we sought. When our proposal was accepted, the project
"Educating for Religious Particularism and Pluralism" was
born. We convened a group of six Catholics and six Jews,
including a few of the participants in the Catholic-Jewish
Colloquium and the addition of academics from both faith traditions whom we believed would be interested in the questions
we were asking.

This group met four times from November 1997 to May
1999 at a conference center near New York City. One of the
initial challenges the group faced was to arrive at working def-
initions of religious particularism and religious pluralism.
Another question that confronted the group was describing
what a religiously pluralistic society might look like and what
would be characteristic of a society committed to religious pluralism.

Most of the November 1997 session was devoted to these
two inquiries, and we emerged with more questions and a
range of issues. Among the more intriguing are the following:

- What is the relationship between pluralism as an
  individual disposition and pluralism as a social/political
  value/affirmation? Is one a prerequisite for the other? Is
  one a context for the other?

- What role might interreligious learning play in
  particularism and pluralism?

- What elements of the particularity of our own traditions
  need to be stressed, enhanced, or developed in order to
  promote a pluralistic orientation?

- What is at stake for each of our traditions and society if
  we do not educate for a renewed understanding of
  particularism and pluralism?

The first meeting of the group sought to lay out a rationale for
concern with particularism and pluralism and to identify con-
textual factors facilitating and hindering receptivity to pluralism. Teams of Catholic and Jewish participants prepared essays
on these issues for the second meeting on May 3–4, 1998. In
addition, one of the Catholic participants presented a paper,
"The Impact of the Unique Relation of Judaism and Christianity
on the Question of Particularism and Pluralism." Members of
the group had expressed an interest in hearing about Christian
and Jewish theologies of religious pluralism. We concluded the
second meeting with some preliminary remarks on theologies of
pluralism. Eventually, we formalized these remarks in a paper
titled "Particularism and Pluralism: A Complicated Clarity"
that the group discussed at its final meeting.

    For our third session on October 18–19, 1998, we invited
two prominent scholars, Rabbi Neil Gillman and Father John
Pawlikowski, to address questions that had emerged in our
previous discussions.[19] Prior to their presentations, we asked
Rabbi Gillman and Father Pawlikowski to listen in on presentations prepared by each of the participants in answer to the
question, "In the face of religious pluralism, what is the
grounding of my own religious particularity?" The opportunity to hear from our participants before they presented
enabled them to have a clearer idea of the thinking of our
group. Too often guest speakers have little opportunity to get
a sense of the group to whom they are speaking.

Then Rabbi Gillman and Father Pawlikowski described the evolution of religious pluralism within their respective faith traditions, identified resources and elements within the traditions that support the value of religious pluralism, and suggested how we might reinterpret those aspects of the traditions that pose barriers to pluralism. Participants had an opportunity to interact with the two scholars and respond to the ideas that were presented.

The final session of the project on May 2–4, 1999, focused on participants' presentations on two questions: "What do you see as the most compelling dimension of religious pluralism and/or the most compelling issue in a theology of pluralism?" and "What would you tell your own community of faith about the value of religious pluralism?" We also sought feedback on the initial draft of the paper, "Particularism and Pluralism: A Complicated Clarity," which we also circulated to a few colleagues in our field. Much of the thinking of that paper is evident in revised form in the first chapter of this book.

This "Educating for Religious Particularism and Pluralism" project was more difficult than the Colloquium, in large measure because we were working with more abstract notions. Nevertheless, interviews conducted in 2005 (which we discuss in chapter 8) document the profound effect the project had on the Catholics and Jews who participated. We decided that it was important to share what the project participants had learned with our colleagues in the Association of Professors and Researchers in Religious Education. Because Sara was the incoming president of APRRE and thus in charge of the program, we invited six members of our group to prepare papers for the annual conference in November 1999 in Toronto.

A sample of group members' comments attests to the power of their experience in the project.

> This was the uniqueness of the Valparaiso experience:
> that it opened the wellsprings to honest sharing, learn-
> ing, and venting; that it removed the walls of separation
> and caution that would deny that what my Catholic
> friends know, feel, and believe can enrich me, as my
> faith, ritual, and story can enrich them; that their deep-
> est beliefs, fears, insecurities, and hopes mirror mine.[20]

The study of texts, particularly Psalms, was an important part
of the educational experience. Over time, it allowed both the
Catholics and the Jews new insights into how each faith understood the meaning of the psalm being read:

> One of the most challenging experiences for me dur-
> ing the Colloquium was studying Psalm 147 with my
> Jewish colleagues…. In verses 7–9, as a Christian I hear
> the voice of the psalmist giving praise for God's univer-
> sal care for humankind. Among Jews, I am reminded of
> a more ordinary, specific kind of care—tufts of pale
> green grass covering the Judean desert hills during the
> rainy season, a harbinger of hope that this year's short
> rainy season would be adequate to supply the water
> needs of the region. Suddenly, God's care is physical,
> concrete, directed to the particular needs of a particu-
> lar people.[21]

When we brought the project to a close in 1999, we pondered
appropriate next steps in promoting interreligious learning in
religious education and as a new way of thinking about interfaith dialogue. In 2000, we submitted another proposal to the
Valparaiso Project on the Education and Formation of People
in Faith for funding to convene a consultation on ideas developed during the previous two projects.

CONSULTATION ON TEACHER PREPARATION FOR EDUCATING FOR RELIGIOUS PARTICULARISM AND PLURALISM

Our hope was to design teacher institutes to influence Catholic and Jewish education, and to explore other ways our thinking on religious particularism and pluralism might be made more widely accessible. We convened selected participants from previous projects and two consultants with expertise in interreligious work on March 11 and 12, 2001. We asked those who had participated in our previous projects to share reflections about what they had learned. One recurring theme was the asymmetry. Not only was the transformative task different for Jews and Catholics, but so, too, was the level of investment. Although many individuals had experienced a transformation, the urgency of new understanding was far less for the Jews than for the Catholics. A different asymmetry arises when it comes to religious pluralism, they told us. While religious pluralism is problematic to a certain extent in both traditions, Judaism starts with the assumption that all humans who obey the basic Noahide moral laws are worthy of redemption, while Catholic teaching has traditionally been more exclusivist with regard to who gets saved, as we discussed in chapter 1. This asymmetry is a challenge when thinking about educating teachers of both traditions in the work of interreligious learning.

Among personal reflections from the March 2001 meeting, Jewish participants reported:

- I had a moment of recognizing that my own experience of God could be changed by interreligious encounter, that my theological experience had the potential to be dramatically changed.

- I developed an ability to identify with the other person's reading of text and tradition so much that you want to preserve it in the other even if it means a certain level of tension.

- I developed an understanding of the language of faith that I just did not have.

- Jews really do not need Christianity to think about and be Jewish ... but it is critical in terms of living in a larger context.

Catholic participants reported:

- There was a turning point when we started to realize that particularism and pluralism are organically related to one another. We had tended to dichotomize.

- I remember a conversation with Danny and that he was one of the first Jews I ever had a conversation with. I was puzzled by people saying Catholics need Jews to understand themselves, but Jews do not need Christians.

- Reality is complicated and our identities are multiple— Catholic, academic, woman, etc. Identity is critical in both our traditions ... and always constituted by relationship with the other.[22]

Consultation participants designed models for three teacher institutes: a multi-year institute for teachers in Catholic and Jewish schools, deemed to be the ideal; a two-day institute with a narrower focus for teachers in Catholic and Jewish schools; and a long-term program for people of both traditions involved in adult education. Among the commonalities in all three designs were the importance of studying texts, sharing ritual and liturgical practices of each tradition, creating a safe environment with skilled facilitators, and confronting the history between Jews and Christians. The thinking behind the designs proved to be important when we had the opportunity to plan and implement two-day institutes for Catholic and Jewish educators, "Interreligious Learning: Christians and Jews Teaching about Each Other."

INTERRELIGIOUS LEARNING WORKSHOPS FOR TEACHERS

These two-day workshops for educators, which we led at Boston College and at Villanova University in June 2002, represented our effort to involve Jews and Catholics in an experience of interreligious learning. We hoped the workshops would sensitize them to the religious other, and to develop new educational insights regarding teaching their own faith and that of the other. From the outset we understood that people brought together for two days could not develop the kind of trust and openness that participants in our longer-term project had experienced. On both occasions, we started with asking the participants to gather in faith-alike groups in order to give them a sense of security in sharing. By asking them to describe what they had learned, formally or informally, about those who were religiously other, we hoped to get at how many of us come with "baggage" of distorted understandings through no fault of our own, but picked up from home, school, church, or synagogue. By inquiring about their present experience, including whether they had personal friendships with people of other religious traditions, we hoped to underline the importance of knowing persons beyond our own religious boundaries.

Based on our earlier work, we also thought it important to expose them to the historical reasons for the tensions that function as "emotional loadings" for any conversation between Christians and Jews. We had prepared a brief presentation on PowerPoint that illumined key historical moments. Two memorable moments emerged from the discussion of that history. One was the discomfort of one of the Catholic participants. Stunned by the church's "teaching of contempt" for Jews and Judaism over its long history, she couldn't quite believe there wasn't a comparable problem in Jewish life. That led to a lively discussion about religions and power. We will never forget the second moment. One of the participants, with tears streaming down his face, quietly remarked: "The church's hostility to Jews over time is so similar to the way it has regarded gays and lesbians." He then "came out" to the group—a revelation even to one of his closest colleagues who had accompanied him to the workshop.

A highlight of these workshops was the attempt to answer "typical" questions Jews and Christians encounter so that participants could understand the complexities hiding behind such questions—and also examine the assumptions lurking within them.

- Why don't Jews believe Jesus is the Messiah?

- Do Christians really believe in the same God as Jews? It seems they believe in three gods.

- If Christians worship the same God as Jews, why do they need Jesus?

- If we worship the same God, why do we do so in such different ways?

- If Jews don't believe in Jesus, can they be saved?

Developing answers to these questions took place in mixed faith groups so that participants could begin to fathom the knowledge requisite for a relatively adequate response.

We also thought it was important to introduce participants to two contemporary statements that respond to the changing relationship between Jews and Christians, *"Dabru Emet"* ("Speaking Truth") and "A Sacred Obligation," written by Jewish and Christian scholars, respectively.[23] By providing the occasion for participants to work their way through these statements, we hoped to offer them language and ideas to use in educating their own communities.

The next opportunity to test out our principles took us to a very different cultural context, the Hong Kong International School (HKIS). It stretched us in new ways.

CONSULTATION AT THE HONG KONG INTERNATIONAL SCHOOL

The Hong Kong International School, a private school of 2,500 students from kindergarten through the secondary level, invited us to be their 2003 Charles W. Dull Visiting Scholars (leading some to call us the "Dull Sisters"!). Founded by the Lutheran Church, Missouri Synod, the school has a longstanding commitment to Christian ideas and values.[24] As the student body became increasingly diverse, many in the faculty and administration struggled with how to fashion a curriculum that honored their Christian heritage and yet respected the religiously variegated backgrounds of their students. The cultural and national origins of the students and their families spanned the globe. The school's mission statement describes it as "an American-style education grounded in the Christian faith and respecting the spiritual lives of all." Given the origins of HKIS, its current social and religious reality, and its commitment to "respecting the spiritual lives of all," the school faced an educational and cultural challenge of remaining true to the Christian tradition of its founding while aspiring to become a school truly reflective of pluralism.

HKIS religion faculty member Lois Voeltz had met Mary Boys at an APRRE meeting some years before, and Mary sent her the paper she had written with Sara Lee on religious particularism and religious pluralism. Based on this work, the faculty and administration invited us to share our wisdom in the hope that it would give them some insight about how to address the potential tension between the particularism of their roots and the pluralism they desired to affirm.

To work as a Jew and a Christian in the multireligious world of Hong Kong challenged us. Hong Kong, a British colony from 1843 to 1997, is a mélange of East and West. A city of about seven million, it is a home to expatriates from all over the world who work in this commercial and financial center. Many of the HKIS students were from expatriate families. Skyscrapers and all the hallmarks of prosperity and Western culture stand side by side with human density that is startling. Temples abound. The Confucian influence is apparent in traditions such as ancestor worship. While a number of HKIS students come from Christian backgrounds (Christians constitute about 10 percent of Hong Kong's population), and a few are Jewish, the student body also reflects Hong Kong's diversity: Buddhists, Taoists, Sikhs, Hindus, and Muslims. A number of students had constructed a multireligious identity, albeit one fairly superficial.

Our visit involved sessions with students, faculty, parents, and administrative staff. In each of these encounters, our objective was to allow participants to share their understanding of their own religious and cultural commitments, and to explore how these commitments are affected by the multicultural realities of Hong Kong. Our consultation opened with our speaking to the entire student body. We confess we were terrified by this, as it had been some time since either of us had worked with adolescents, let alone eight hundred at a time. In preparing for this occasion, we had asked the religion teachers to invite students to formulate questions they hoped we might address. Among other questions, we learned that many students were surprised that a Catholic and a Jew could work together and esteem each other's faith, respecting the truth claims of the other's tradition. In fact, many students felt that religious differences were responsible for much of the evil in the world, so they preferred to think of themselves as having no serious religious identity.

In a workshop with the faculty, we asked them to analyze one of their own curricular standards: "Students examine the life of Jesus and articulate and interpret the Christian story as seen through the Old and New Testaments." We asked them to reflect on how the religious diversity of the school affected their implementation of this standard in light of the mission statement. Certainly, this was an appropriate standard for HKIS, but precisely *how* various teachers chose to implement it was the key variable. In order to open discussion about what it means to teach a core belief of Christianity in a heterogeneous environment, we used clips from an excellent film, *Jews and Christians: A Journey of Faith.*[25] A lively discussion ensued. Then, after doing a presentation about our understanding of key terms, such as pluralism and diversity, particularism, relativism and fundamentalism, we led a two-part closing exercise. We first asked the faculty about their own stance: "If you have a commitment to religious pluralism, what implications follow for engaging the religious 'other'?" Finally, we asked faculty members working in table groups to create guidelines for themselves and their students that would help them engage with religious others.

During our week at HKIS, we attempted to analyze the complex theological challenges involved in the school's mission statement in relation to the curriculum. By working as systematically as we could to show the depth of the issues, we hoped to reassure those who might be fearful of change and to provide some resources to stimulate their rethinking. When we met with parents, we had them participate in an interreligious learning experience. We then asked them to assess the value of the experience and to speculate on what it might mean to create such experiences at HKIS.

We were privileged to meet so many talented, dedicated educators who were willing to confront the complex problem of particularism and pluralism. At best, we helped them identify questions they would need to address in order to be loyal to their Lutheran roots, to fashion a curriculum honoring the diversity of the students, and to prepare them to function intelligently in a religiously pluralistic world. During our week at HKIS, we witnessed dedication to serious philosophical and ideological wrestling with difficult questions. We could feel some of the tensions as the administration and faculty struggled to be true to their religious commitments and move toward an authentically pluralistic community in all aspects of the day-to-day life of the school.

We returned to the United States knowing that we had merely opened up some lines of thought, yet grateful for gaining a new perspective on the issue of religious particularism and pluralism. Although we have not been able to stay in contact with school administrators since our visit, we are in touch with two of the faculty leaders from that period, Lois Voeltz and Jan Westrick, both of whom have returned to the United States and are writing a book about their efforts.

In describing our major projects, we have sought to highlight the major contours, show a sampling of the questions we offered for discussion, and report some of what participants said. What we are less skilled at describing is the profound effect these participants have had on us. It is they who have inspired this book and given us such hope that, amid all the tensions in our world, so many people are dedicated to drawing upon their religious traditions as a source of reconciliation.

We turn now to the educational convictions and principles that serve as the foundation for interreligious teaching and learning.

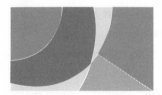

5

Toward a Theory of Interreligious Teaching and Learning

Having described in the previous chapter some of our collaborative projects, here we will go backstage, as it were, to explore some of the convictions and principles that inform our work. By explaining our assumptions, philosophy, and methods, we hope to enhance the possibilities for others to draw from, adapt, and build upon our work in designing and leading interreligious dialogue. Thus, we will also refer to educational literature that is valuable for planning, leading, and evaluating interreligious exchange, especially in North American cultures.

COLLEGIAL TEACHING

Over the course of our long collaboration, we simply took it for granted that we would teach together in various ways. In retrospect, we see that it is vital to have leaders from each tradition who trust and respect each other. This "collegial teaching" is indeed dialogue done in the presence of the other. Even when we are separated by many miles, "we formulate our hypotheses and draw our conclusions in the presence of the other, whether at any given moment that presence be actual, anticipated, or imagined."[1]

Collegial teaching in any context depends on mutual respect, common goals, and joint preparation. In the context of an interreligious program, where both leaders and participants must deal with the uniqueness of the other and the other's tradition, trust, honesty, and willingness to support one another are critical. Over the years, our continuing conversations have affirmed that it is acceptable, even desirable, to ask hard questions about one another's tradition and contemporary community. Our conversations underscore the importance of honesty in interreligious learning.

Over the years we have developed a close friendship, but it is not the most important aspect of our work. Rather, two elements we share are more significant. First, each of us is deeply committed to her religious tradition and continuously seeks to learn more of its depth and breadth. As different as Jews and Christians are, we recognize in one another's religious practices and beliefs many common hopes and obligations. We share the realization that "genuine faith in God is incompatible with the absolutizing of anything other than God, including a cherished tradition that exists to foster faith in God."[2] Moreover, having worked professionally in the church and synagogue for much of our lives, we are mindful of the hypocrisies and finitude of institutional religion. We consider ourselves loyal critics who love our traditions, even as we sometimes feel betrayed by them. In desiring that our own traditions might flourish, we have come to desire the flourishing of the other's.

Second, each of us is an experienced teacher who has come to our interreligious work steeped in educational literature. The compatibility of our educational philosophies contributes immeasurably to the ease with which we work together, both in the planning process and in the various sessions and their evaluation. We are both, for reasons that will become evident in this chapter, "process persons" who pay careful attention to designing programs that involve persons in active learning. We bring fundamental convictions about teaching to our work, which we will lay out in the first major section of this chapter. Through our collaboration, we have developed principles of interreligious learning, the focus of the second major section of this chapter.

Those who lead interreligious encounter will come with their own strengths. As valuable as we have found our experience as educators to be, the sine qua non for interreligious leadership is knowledgeable commitment to one's own religious tradition and respect for the other's. We hope those with less background in education will find this chapter a guide for their own leadership.

FUNDAMENTAL CONVICTIONS ABOUT TEACHING

Over the years, we have developed three fundamental convictions about teaching, which we outline here, and then develop briefly in narrative:

Teaching is a complex activity that entails:

- Establishing a hospitable environment

- Inviting interaction

- Posing questions

- Identifying appropriate resources

- Listening

- Leading learning activities

- Helping persons become agents of their own learning

Teaching requires painstaking preparation that includes:

- Identifying and refining learning goals in relation to the needs of learners

- Plotting the general flow of thought

- Selecting the most effective pedagogical strategy

- Making resources accessible

- Structuring creative learning activities

- Formulating effective questions

- Anticipating necessary adaptations

- Reflecting in retrospect

Teaching is a profoundly relational art that requires:

- Creating a safe and stimulating environment for learning

- Honoring each person's dignity and capacity to learn

- Challenging persons tactfully

Teaching is not to be confused with telling or technique, though both are used. Teaching is a complex activity that involves hospitality above all. This includes creating an environment that invites interaction, posing involving questions, identifying available resources, and leading engaging learning activities. It also means practicing the art of listening. Appropriately, two of the books on Mary's syllabus at Union for her course "The Practices of Teaching" are *Learning to Listen, Learning to Teach* and *Teaching with Your Mouth Shut.*

Of course, teaching requires knowledge. There is no substitute for knowing one's subject; constant study is indispensable. Teaching always is a fruit of a teacher's study, a teacher's poring over the material to seek knowledge and wisdom. But that does not imply that teaching should be the *infusion* of the knowledge the teacher has assimilated. Teaching entails far more than imparting knowledge, which, in the memorable metaphor of Paulo Freire, is "banking education." In banking education, the teacher "deposits" information in learners, who are expected merely to "receive, retain, and return" that information. To teach as a depositor impedes the transformative possibilities of education because it fosters passivity rather than agency. Education needs to be, in Freire's term, "problem-posing"—that is, participants need to be engaged with issues, not merely be passive recipients of the teacher's knowledge.[3]

Because we desire to transform the ways Jews and Christians understand each other, it is vital that we involve them in the transformative process. We agree with philosopher of education Nicholas Burbules that "in pedagogical encounters, we do not change other people. They change themselves. They construct their own understandings, they change their minds, they decide on alternative courses of action, they redefine their priorities, and so on."[4] Beginning from this perspective, Burbules argues, shapes an essentially different teaching stance. This is often termed a "constructivist" approach to learning. As Burbules describes it, this approach is "defined less by 'giving' students certain things, 'shaping' students in particular ways, or 'leading' them to particular conclusions." Rather, a constructivist approach is characterized by "creating opportunities and occasions in which students will, given their own questions, needs, and purposes, gradually construct a more mature understanding of themselves, the world, and others—an understanding that, *by definition*, must be their own."[5] Thus, the leaders' task is to design sessions that require involvement and contribute to participants' becoming the agents of their own learning. This does not preclude lecturing, but means that every presentation must include an opportunity to "take on" what has been said. It also means that discussions must be calibrated in such a way that participants feel a stake in their outcome.

If we hope to transcend mere telling in teaching, then painstaking preparation is critical for both leaders and participants. Neophyte teachers are often amazed that teaching requires so much preparation. While effective teaching is typically associated with what transpires in the pedagogical setting, preparation, largely hidden from view, is vital. It includes activities such as specifying clear goals, being clear about the logic, organizing appropriate resources, structuring creative learning activities, formulating thought-provoking questions, and anticipating possible adaptations in response to the interests, backgrounds and needs of diverse learners. Preparation also has a retrospective phase that includes reflecting after a pedagogical encounter on better ways of making the material accessible and on what might be done differently the next time.

Those who lead an educational event, however, are not the only ones who must prepare. So, too, must the participants if they are to take ownership of the ideas under examination. Thus, whenever possible, we ask participants to come to sessions having read specific texts, for example, and having formulated an initial response to open-ended questions. Although it is not possible in every situation to have opportunity beforehand to contact participants, prior information about content, goals, and method allows participants to come with at least some preliminary considerations. For us, preparing a session includes consideration of what will be most valuable for participants to prepare. Giving persons a "heads up" before an event, even by electronic mail, helps them enter the educational process more quickly and fully.

Yet preparation is not all, because teaching is a profoundly relational art that requires interpersonal intelligence.[6] As a relationship, teaching involves vulnerability, in part because it challenges our parochialisms. Over the course of many years of teaching, we have often been humbled by seeing some of our own assumptions exploded by those who come from "places" (whether geographical, cultural, ethnic, racial, or religious) different from our own. We have a vivid memory, for example, of planning a session for the Catholic-Jewish Colloquium on the ways in which the immigrant status of both Jews and Catholics once made us "outsiders" in the United States—only to be chastened by an African-American participant, who rightly upbraided us for forgetting that her ancestors had been forcibly brought across the Atlantic as slaves. In Hong Kong, we found some of our assumptions tested by the syncretistic backgrounds of many of the students who, having lived in two or three different cultures in their young lives, had constructed a religious identity upon diverse beliefs and practices.

In teaching, we encounter "strangers" who may cause us disequilibrium. As uncomfortable as that can be, we have come to see that the encounter with the stranger is fundamental to the educational processes. Dwayne Huebner, an educational philosopher who was one of Mary's mentors, rightly speaks of education as the "meeting of the historically determined self with the new, the strange, the stranger" in such a way that the profound longing and thirst central to human life are "recognized as the source and goal of life." He adds that encounters with strangers are all the more important in the religious realm because they are "pathways to new understandings of how God and human beings are in relationship."[7]

So teaching involves a large dose of risk. It is, in Joseph McDonald's terms, an "uncertain craft" that involves "a wild triangle of relations—among teacher, students, subject—and the points of this triangle shift continuously," making "multiple small certainties" arise.[8] Meticulous preparation, however requisite, is no assurance of success; no matter how skilled, experienced, or charismatic the teacher, she or he can never be completely in control of the variables. Stephen Brookfield observes, "As teachers we cross the borders of chaos to inhabit zones of ambiguity. For every event in which we feel things are working out as we anticipated they would, there is an event that totally confounds our expectations."[9]

All this can heighten vulnerability, especially in the already charged climate of interreligious dialogue. Thus, it is crucial that leaders develop a contemplative spirit that sustains them amid the complexity and inspires them to restrain their own ego needs. Teaching demands "a sturdy self on the part of the teacher, combined 'with a yielding and receptive character of soul' incompatible with undue concern for self-protection of advancement."[10] It is crucial to remember that as teachers we are facilitators of a learning process and not the center of attention.

PRINCIPLES OF INTERRELIGIOUS LEARNING

In the first chapter we briefly discussed a term we began using in the mid-1990s to describe our work: interreligious learning. Interreligious learning is a form of dialogue that emphasizes study in the presence of the religious other and an encounter with the tradition that the other embodies. In the process of reflecting on and writing about the Catholic-Jewish Colloquium, we identified convictions that we have now developed as four principles of interreligious learning. As in the previous section, we first offer an outline and then develop the principles in the narrative.

Interreligious Learning Is

a form of interreligious dialogue emphasizing study in the presence of the religious other and encounter with the tradition the other embodies.

1. Study in the presence of the other is fundamental to interreligious learning.
2. Process is the key element in all interreligious learning. Content and process must be inextricably connected.
3. The leaders must provide the environment, experiences, and resources to enable participants to risk crossing religious borders and integrate their learning into their own religious identity.
4. Interreligious learning necessitates helping participants "get inside" the religious tradition of the other.

In claiming that study in the presence of the other is the fundamental principle of interreligious learning, we define "study" broadly. "Study" means not simply poring over texts but encompassing conversations that open up new perspectives or draw participants more deeply into thought. Michael Oakeshott appropriately depicts conversation as an "unrehearsed intellectual venture."[11]

Interreligious learning brings out the complexity of issues in encountering another tradition and the obligation to respond thoughtfully and reverently. The "presence of others" in our projects was indeed physical—in the same location—but presence need not be limited to this, since many who participated in our projects report the lasting effects of the sessions on their lives even when separated by spatial distance. For instance, one of the Catholic participants in the Colloquium wrote to us a year or so later: "On [this first] day of Passover, I feel compelled to remember by recalling each name and face of each Jewish member of the Colloquium as she or he gathered with family and friends to commemorate a night different from all other nights. Passover is now different for me."[12] Significant encounters with the religious other make for a lingering presence.

Both of us have been to sessions advertised as "dialogues" when those who attend have virtually no opportunity to interact with each other, or even the opportunity to learn the names of those around them. Merely listening to the same speaker or panel of speakers and having opportunity to ask questions after the presentation might at best constitute a prelude to dialogue. What happens *after* the speaker or film is the moment of interreligious learning.

Interreligious learning aims to go deeper by fostering relationships *among* participants, and *with* key texts, practices, and beliefs of the other's tradition. By structuring the study so that it happens in the presence of the other, we seek to enable participants to construct a common body of knowledge even as they hear diverse interpretations. By including community-building and opportunity for sharing in depth, we hope to honor the *formative dimension of the educational* process, that is, the emotional, intellectual, psychic, and spiritual dimensions of learning. Gathering a group simply to hear lectures—even brilliant ones—does not have the same effect.

Transformation happens *through dialogue for which there is preparation, resources, and support,* and through experiencing a religious tradition *as embodied in the other,* whether in formal study sessions or at table or in late-night conversations.

Transformation, however, cannot be predicted; it is one of the variables that leaders do not control. Interreligious learning affects many aspects of an individual's religious self-understanding and identity in ways that cannot readily be anticipated. For example, one of the fundamental axioms of our Jewish-Christian work is that Jews don't so much have to change their theology as they do their self-understanding based on history. Christians, on the other hand, have to reconstitute their theology because so much of it is grounded in an inadequate understanding of Judaism. Thus, in preparing for various sessions, we have generally worked from the assumption that participants from each of the traditions have different issues to address. The interreligious learning experience will have its greatest impact on that issue of religious identity most challenged by confrontation with the other tradition.

So in encountering a vibrant Judaism, as affirmed and lived by Jewish participants, Christians typically need to address serious questions about the validity of a theology in which Judaism has been superseded by Christianity. Jews, for whom Christianity poses no apparent theological challenge, typically need to confront how much of Jewish identity has been shaped by identifying as a victim, particularly of Christian persecutions. In reality, while these changes do, in fact, take place in our sessions, we have sometimes been surprised by other changes in self-understanding. In the Catholic-Jewish Colloquium, for example, we found that Jews, who came with a heightened sense of their difference from Christians, began to talk of their connection to Christianity. Catholics, conscious of their tradition's grounding in Judaism, began to speak of the distinctiveness of Judaism. Learning about the tradition of the other in the presence of the other led to both a sharpening and a diminishing of similarities and differences between the two traditions in the perception of the participants. Perhaps because the Colloquium took place over an extended time and enabled participants to probe more deeply, we found that Jews became more involved in theological issues and Catholics far more sensitive to the historical origins of Christianity and to their largely tragic historical relationship with Jews.

It should come as no surprise that interreligious learning involves unanticipated changes in understanding and feeling among the participants. Questions raised in serious interreligious encounter are by no means predictable. Moreover, such questions challenge people of faith in unsettling ways, because the "stranger" may pose questions in unfamiliar terms. A memorable example is the time a Jewish participant asked the Catholic members of the Colloquium, "Why do you need Jesus? Isn't God enough?" The Catholics, normally a voluble group, sat in stunned silence for a time. Finally, one of the members ventured, "It is not that we need him. It is just that he is." This response, however inadequate, set off a conversation that continues to this day; none of us present that day has ever forgotten it. Interreligious learning in an environment of study, support, and sharing promotes religious growth in the face of these questions, not a crisis of faith.

Process is the key element in all interreligious learning. Leaders are catalysts for people to engage with ideas, questions, and issues in ways that enable them to enter into those ideas at every level of their being. The key is that content and process are inextricably connected. So when we prepare for our various sessions—whether a multi-session event such as the Catholic-Jewish Colloquium, or the various groups with whom we met in Hong Kong, or a one-day workshop—we work in ways shaped, in part, by a model of "pedagogical reasoning and action." In so doing, we draw from Lee Shulman, a highly regarded educational theorist who has influenced us both.

Shulman's model begins with the teacher's comprehension of the subject matter in relation to the larger purposes of the situation and the discipline. In studying or "comprehending," which we often do together, we are involved in identifying what we find to be compelling in the subject matter, that which seemingly asks itself to be taught. This phase is generally time-consuming. We are not seeking "mastery" of the topics, but searching for key concepts in relation to the context of the subject matter and the situation in which we will be working. In other words, to be knowledgeable requires more than grasping a great deal of information; it requires being "caught up" in the transforming possibilities of this knowledge.

A major component of Shulman's model is the phase he terms "transformation" (and that we call preparation), consisting of four movements:

- Preparation: This involves study of the logic and insights of the content, whether texts or other source material, with an eye toward connecting these texts with the "big picture," and specifying goals for the various sessions.

- Representation: This demands thinking about how to make the subject matter accessible in vivid ways. A sign Mary once saw in a fabric store aptly expresses this pedagogical challenge: "Materialize your ideas."

- Selection: This presumes that the educational leader has a repertoire of teaching strategies. Among the teacher's various strategies, which is most appropriate for the particular ideas and issues at hand?

- Adaptation: This demands consideration of the subject matter and strategies in light of what the participants are likely to come with in terms of prior knowledge, possible misconceptions, cultural background, and special needs and interests.

Only then is one ready to teach, although "ready" is a relative term—no matter how much preparation we have done, we never feel quite ready! Nevertheless, as Margret Buchmann says, "uncertainty and imperfection are overtaken by the need to act."[13]

There are still other moments of preparation in Shulman's model. During the sessions themselves, evaluation is happening constantly: leaders take measure both informally and formally of participants' learning, as well as the effectiveness of their own teaching. All this becomes the data for a new round of preparation through reflection and return to the subject matter in light of all that has happened; thus, it becomes a source for further comprehension. Teaching is appropriately thought of as "reflection-in-action" and "action-in-reflection."[14]

The following table summarizes Shulman's model, though by summarizing it in table form we risk making pedagogical reasoning and action appear more linear and neater than it is in flesh-and-blood situations. Nevertheless, we have found Shulman to be an excellent guide in thinking through the various phases in teaching.

SHULMAN'S MODEL OF PEDAGOGICAL REASONING AND ACTION[15]

Comprehension

- Understanding purposes, subject matter structures, ideas within and outside the discipline

Transformation

- *Preparation*: Critical interpretation and analysis of texts, structuring and segmenting, development of curricular repertoire, and clarification of purposes

- *Representation*: Use of a representational repertoire, which includes analogies, metaphors, examples, demonstrations, and explanations

- *Selection*: Choice from among an instructional repertoire, which includes modes of teaching, organizing, managing, and arranging

- *Adaptation and Tailoring to Student Characteristics*: Consideration of conceptions, preconceptions, misconceptions, and difficulties; language, culture, and motivations; social class, gender, age, ability, aptitude, interests, self-concepts, and attention

Instruction

- Including management, presentations, interactions, group work, discipline, humor, questioning, and other aspects of active teaching, discovery, or inquiry instruction

Evaluation

- Checking for student understanding during interactive teaching

- "Testing" student understanding at the end of the lesson or units

- Evaluating one's own performance, and adjusting for experiences

Reflection

- Reviewing, reconstructing, reenacting, and critically analyzing one's own and the class's performance, and grounding explanations in evidence

New Comprehensions

- Understanding purposes, subject matter, students, teaching, and self

- Consolidating new understandings and learnings from experience

We have consistently employed Shulman's model of pedagogical reasoning and action in our work. For example, in thinking through the first meeting of the Colloquium, we decided it was important to devote one of its five sessions to the distinctive ways Jews and Christians interpret scripture. When we studied together in the preparatory phase, we did a considerable amount of thinking aloud about the most important elements in the way each tradition interpreted scripture, at times consulting various secondary sources. Out of this conversation we eventually arrived at the conceptual focus for the two-hour session: *Jewish and Christian communities may read the same text in distinctive ways because biblical texts have multiple meanings that are shaped, in large part, by historical experience and theological traditions.*

We moved from this concept to the phase of representation when we chose a text important to both our traditions, Genesis 22 (the *Akedah*, or "Binding of Isaac") as a case in point. Then we researched and compiled commentaries that would illustrate our point, selecting several for inclusion in a packet to distribute to participants. Once we had these in hand, we moved to the selection of teaching strategies. In brief, our strategy was as follows:

- After reading Genesis 22, Sara posed two questions to participants: 1) When you teach this text, what do you teach and why? 2) How do you feel about this text?

- Mary then led the group in looking at New Testament references to this passage (Romans 8:32, James 2:21–23, and Hebrews 11:17–19), because these allusions and references influenced the commentaries of early church writers.

- The two of us then distributed the packet of selected commentaries from early Jewish literature and early church writings. We asked participants to identify the major emphasis of each commentary, and listed those on the board.

- We then posed this question for discussion in small groups: "How is each tradition reading Genesis 22, and why?"

- We moved to interpretation of Genesis 22 in poetry and drama by incorporating readings from a twelfth-century liturgical poem by Rabbi Ephraim ben Jacob of Bonn, "The *Akedah*" and a [Christian] medieval mystery play on Abraham and Isaac (in the Brome cycle of mystery plays), which a few participants had prepared as a reader's theater.

- We concluded the session by asking: "How do you feel about the way our communities have used this text?"

Throughout this exercise, we were mindful of adaptations that needed to be made. In some instances, this meant clarifying terms we anticipated would be unfamiliar, such as a commentary on Genesis 22 from a Targum, a paraphrase of a Hebrew text in Aramaic. Since understanding typology was fundamental to this exercise and was likely to be unfamiliar to some, we clarified its meaning as we went through the various commentaries from early church writers such as Irenaeus, Tertullian, and Origen.[16]

This was a modest exercise, designed to give participants a sense of one way that the other tradition interprets scripture. It built upon the previous session, in which participants shared sacred texts central to their identity as a Jew or Catholic and examined the differing canons of our traditions. Mindful that this was only the second day in which participants had gathered, we sought to formulate our questions in ways that allowed for differences to surface without being judged.

The Shulman model might seem a bit daunting to some. Joseph McDonald's more colorfully formulated questions get at some of the same concerns. He asks:

- "What shall I teach amid all that I might teach?"

- "How can I grasp it myself so that my grasping may enable theirs?"

- "What are they thinking and feeling—toward me, toward each other, toward the thing I am trying to teach?"

- "How near should I come, how far off should I stay? How much clutch, how much gas?"[17]

McDonald's questions lead us to reflect on specific elements of the process we find so critical to interreligious learning: the role of discussion, the crafting of questions, the place of conversation, and the formulation of learning tasks.

DISCUSSION, QUESTIONING, AND CONVERSATION

One of the constant "clutch and gas" tensions is the role of discussion, which Stephen Brookfield, a preeminent theorist of adult education, defines as "purposeful conversation and deliberation."[18] All of us have experienced discussions that lacked direction and wasted valuable time—in effect, shared ignorance. Nevertheless, we affirm with Brookfield, that

> discussion groups are irreplaceable in the learning of adults.... Lectures, demonstrations, independent study ... are all useful techniques by means of which information can be assimilated and a grasp of fundamentals can be acquired. But it is when one's nascent, inchoate ideas and concepts are tested out in the company of others that a certain creative tension comes into play.[19]

For us, the heart of discussion is posing thought-provoking questions. More than once we have worked for hours to pose the best questions possible only to have one of us get up the next morning and say, "I've thought of another way to ask that." Back we go to the drawing board, trying to get just the right wording. However tedious this might feel at the time, the chance to revisit our formulation results in better-crafted questions and thus generally in livelier, deeper discussions—although even the most artfully worded questions do not guarantee a great discussion.

So for us, much of the pedagogy of the phase of transformation (in Shulman's model) involves posing good questions, that is, open-ended questions that invite reflection, synthesis, and creativity. We aim for quality rather than quantity; we are looking for a few good questions rather many mediocre ones. We avoid questions that simply return data to us, because we want to encourage thinking that transcends mere comprehension.[20]

The kinds of questions we pose depend on what we hope to accomplish in a given session. If it is our hope simply to introduce and orient a group, we might ask questions such as the following we posed to a group of Christians and Jews in two-day workshops at Boston College and Villanova University in 2002. We initially had them meet in "faith-alike groups" of four people to discuss:

- What did you learn (whether explicitly or implicitly) as a child about the religious belief and practice of those neighbors and schoolmates who were religiously "other"?

- To what degree in your own religious education was there any attention to systematic learning about those who were religiously other?

- To what extent did you or do you have any significant friendships with people of other religious traditions? What difference does it make to your own religious self-understanding?

After participants had an opportunity to address these questions in their small groups, we asked them to draw some generalizations that might be shared with all the participants. Note that these questions, while eliciting personal experience from discussants, did not involve judgment. One may, for example, have heard as a child a negative or stereotypical comment about another's religion or ethnicity, but this fact is not the fault of the person. Rather, it is a piece of information about the context in which he or she was socialized. Or perhaps what might have been taught in the formal context of religious schooling was counterbalanced by what was conveyed in the home. We hoped that the third question would invite reflection about the impact of friendship across religious borders; we anticipated that some might not have such friendships, yet would not be embarrassed to admit this in a small group.

Good discussions often flow from stimulating resource materials. For example, on the second day of the workshop, we worked with two recent statements on Jewish-Christian relations, *"Dabru Emet"* and *"A Sacred Obligation"* (see appendices 1 and 2). Four Jewish scholars authored the former, and the Christians Scholars Group on Christian-Jewish Relations (the ecumenical group referred to in chapter 3) wrote the latter. In both cases, the authors intended the statements to stimulate conversation within their own traditions regarding relationship with the other. Because we wanted both to disseminate these statements and to open participants to their potential as resources for their communities, we focused on their educational challenges. We again began in "faith-alike" groups, asking each tradition to read the statement addressed to their own community and then answer the following questions:

- In terms of the statement addressed to your community, what would you personally affirm most strongly, and where do you have some hesitations and disagreements?

- How do you think the public of your faith tradition with whom you are involved would respond to this statement?

- What kind of educational challenges do these statements and the likely response to them in your community represent?

We then asked each group to report to the rest of the participants regarding the second and third questions. We concluded the session with participants assigned to "mixed-faith" groups of five and asked: "What are the educational challenges for your tradition delineated in the 'other's' statement?"

However important it is to pose questions in ways that will serve the discussion, questions are never ends in themselves. Rather, they are stimuli for learning and the foundation for good conversation. And in interreligious exchange, good conversation is vital if participants are to engage differences.

It might appear that differences are best dealt with through argumentation, that seemingly more rigorous exercise of logic and rationality. Argument does have its uses in interreligious encounter, but it is a far less valuable resource than conversation. Argument can all too easily focus on winning rather than on understanding. Argument, as philosopher of education Margret Buchmann points out, involves contestants, whereas conversation involves partners. What makes conversation so useful, Buchmann says, is its "reciprocal quality, breadth of subject matter, the room it gives to different voices, and the delightful turns it may take. Conversations have flexible rules of relevance and evidence. All manner of impressions, ideas, and experience can enter." As she points out, "ideals of perfection in clarity and coherence" are not as important in conversation as in argument. Thus, "one may get answers to questions one never thought of asking (but ought to have asked) or have one's answers answered. Yet conversation is not mere talk; it can include argument and has its own logical postulates."[21]

Of course, as Buchmann reminds us, conversation is educative only when the conversation partners already know something—

knowledge of self, as well as the subject at hand. Hence, conversations must be stimulated with excellent resources and questions that demand thought.

LEARNING TASKS

We have found that involving participants in "learning tasks" is one of the most helpful means of stimulating and sustaining lively conversations. It is the leader's task to design activities that enable participants to "get inside" the issues or concepts. For example, if one of the objectives is for participants to understand ways the other's religious tradition functions in their lives, we might ask them to gather first in "faith-alike" groups to address what they would most like the other to know about them, and then to share with the other group. Or if the objective is for participants to identify how perspective shapes our understanding of polemic in sacred texts, they might be asked to read the Gospel of Matthew from two points of view: from the perspective that sees Matthew as writing his Gospel as a Jew trying to convince other Jews that Jesus is the true Torah, or as a "Christian" taking issue with Judaism.

Learning tasks, according to Jane Vella, an adult educator who has taught all over the world, are part of a seven-phase process of educational design that she sums up as: *who* (participants), *why* (context), *when* (time), *where* (site), *what* (content), *what for* (objectives), and *how* (learning tasks). Learning tasks address the question of "how" the objectives—the "what for"—will be addressed. One of the most valuable aspects of her seven steps of planning is the way in which she shows the importance of specificity in connecting all phases of the design, but especially in linking the "what?," the "what for?," and the "how?" The educational leader's role is to give access to the content, which includes knowledge, skills, and attitudes, by way of identifying detailed "achievement-based objectives" that can in turn be met through learning tasks. An "achievement-based objective" is far from a poetic term, but it challenges leaders to name specific outcomes of a session.[22]

To play out Vella's seven-steps of planning:

Who? A group of Jewish and Christian educators, all of whom have a graduate degree in some aspect of theology, Jewish studies, or religious education.

Why? They want to understand the role the New Testament may play in fostering or hindering relations between Jews and Christians in our time.

When? A two-hour session held in the evening.

Where? At a neutral site, a conference center.

What? The Gospel of Matthew in its first-century context and twenty-first-century understanding.

What for? By the end of this session, (1) participants will have examined specific passages from the Gospel of Matthew, (2) analyzed alternative theories regarding Matthew's relationship with Judaism, and (3) discussed the significance of these theories for interpreting his Gospel today.

How? (1) Read together these passages: Matthew 6:1–5, 23:1–33, and 27:25; (2) access specified links for brief commentaries on these passages (this assumes a site that has Internet access; if not, then these commentaries might be provided ahead of time); and (3) respond in your working group to the following question: "What difference does it make to the interpretation of Matthew's Gospel today whether we regard him as still within the Jewish community in composing his account or as having broken with it?"

A commitment to process in interreligious encounters is labor-intensive; it demands rigorous planning. In the end, however, we believe the work is immensely worthwhile because it invites participants to involve themselves in learning. Process has another dimension: it fosters relationships that may linger long after a session ends.

In interreligious encounter, the leaders must provide the environment, conditions, experiences, and resources to enable participants to take up the challenges and risks of crossing religious borders and integrating their learning into their religious self-identity. Put another way, leadership in interreligious education requires attention to the safety of the participants. Participants (and leaders) bring their own insecurities, and encounter between religious groups is often freighted with centuries or more of ignorance and intolerance. In our work, it is crucial that we factor in the effects of the long history of Christian disparagement of Judaism and vilification of Jews. This history typically makes Jews wary of Christians, the more powerful religious majority since the late fourth century. Christians often know Judaism only in the abstract and generally accompanied by many misconceptions, so they may be uneasy in the presence of "real" Jews (no longer only "Hebrews" of old). If genuine exchange is to take place, then leaders must make the safety of the participants a priority. That is, participants must be assured that the educational experience will be for their benefit.

Jane Vella suggests five elements of a safe educational environment:

- Participants trust in the competence of the educational design and the competence of the leaders.

- Participants trust in the feasibility and relevance of the objectives.

- Participants find their voice through conversation in small groups.

- Participants trust in the sequence of activities, moving from relatively easy to more complex tasks.

- Participants experience affirmation and lack of judgment.

"Teachers," Vella says, "do not empower adult learners; they encourage the use of the power that learners were born with."[23]

One of the competencies that leaders must have in structuring a safe environment is sensitivity to symbols. For example, the cross is one of the most precious and prevalent symbols of Christianity. Yet it often evokes negative reactions for Jews because they have suffered so much from accusations that they were "Christ-killers." Whenever we have control over decisions about environment (and the requisite funds), we prefer to work in a neutral space rather than in an institution under Christian sponsorship that would have either a crucifix or a cross hung in many rooms.[24] Safety also requires attention to details that makes taking risks more feasible. For us, this includes attention to dietary norms and refraining from common worship. Most Jews are uncomfortable with common worship, though by the end of the Catholic-Jewish Colloquium, participants asked whether we might include opportunity to worship together.

When safety is not factored in, it can have disastrous effects. Mary once witnessed this in a weekend gathering about fifteen years ago of thirty Jewish, Christian, and Muslim "women of faith." At one point, participants were asked to gather in their respective traditions and to list five stereotypes about the other. When the groups returned to the plenary, they were asked to read out their list—and immediately tension filled the air as people rose to denounce the stereotype and defend their tradition. Mary wondered, "What in the world were the leaders thinking?" By encouraging participants to list stereotypes, the leaders had inadvertently opened up old wounds. She remembers "willing" the clock to move to the close of the event!

Interreligious learning necessitates helping participants "get inside" the religious tradition of the other so that they see the other tradition as offering a living, vital way of life. One of the most important aspects of this is encouraging participants to give voice to those "affective attachments" that root them deeply in their tradition. By learning what binds each to her or his tradition, the religious other gains insight into its compelling power. So among the learning tasks should be those that allow participants to share aspects of their tradition that they personally find powerful. For example, one of the most effective learning tasks we designed was to invite persons to come to a session with two selections from their sacred texts, one that they thought was central to the tradition itself, and a second that they found personally most meaningful. Another especially valuable learning task was asking persons to share an aspect of their holidays/liturgical seasons that was most evocative for them. We simply listened in those sessions—and witnessed how moved everyone was. Similarly, on several occasions we have organized a session around a particular psalm and have been struck by the depth of the ensuing discussion.

Such sharing of a person's deep connection to his or her own tradition is particularly significant when the traditions have a history of conflict. For example, because Jews have suffered so much from Christians, it may be difficult for them to appreciate what discipleship to the Way of Jesus means. When, however, they come to know Christians who are committed to lives of justice and reconciliation, they gain a very different perspective on Christianity. Likewise, Christians who may have grown up with notions of Judaism as legalistic find themselves with a deepened appreciation for this tradition when they see the vitality of Jewish life.

Our many years in classrooms and our long collaboration affirm Stephen Brookfield's observation: "Teaching and learning are such complex processes, and teachers and learners are such complex beings that no model of practice or pedagogical approach will apply in all settings."[25] What we have attempted in this chapter is to open up the convictions and theories that we have found so helpful in planning, leading, and evaluating interreligious learning. We hope it will be of value to our readers.

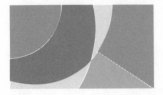

6

After Auschwitz: Conversations in a Krakow Park

"Hell on earth" is one of the phrases most often used to describe Auschwitz. Why, then, did we choose to go there, why in the presence of the other, and what insights has our journey led to thus far?

A CONVERSATION BEGUN: MARY

Odd as it may seem, I don't think I ever clearly articulated my reasons for going to Auschwitz, even to myself. In retrospect, I see how the desire grew from cumulative experience: immersing myself in the long history between Jews and Christians, participating in many Jewish-Christian dialogues over the years, meeting survivors and coming to know their children and grandchildren, working with colleagues committed to the study of and teaching about the Shoah, and struggling with the evil that comes from treating humans as "other" and "inferior." Insofar as Auschwitz has become the preeminent symbol of human evil, I somehow had to stand there myself.[1]

I felt compelled to acknowledge what it represented, not only as a site of Nazi atrocities, but as a "killing field" made fertile in part by anti-Jewish teaching of my own church. Going to Auschwitz was in some small and mysterious way an act of penitence. If "no one is permitted to pass by the tragedy of the Shoah," then going to Auschwitz was one way of honoring the obligation to take a long look at it.[2]

Although I may not have been explicit about my reasons for going to Auschwitz, one aspect of the trip was clear from the start: I wanted to go with Sara. It seemed a natural outcome of our professional and personal relationship of nearly twenty years. Sara's only stipulation was that we also visit Prague as a way of complementing the emotional drain of visiting the camps with the delight of touring a magnificent city.

When I mentioned to a close friend, Lesley Sacouman, who is also a member of the religious congregation to which I belong, that we intended to go to Auschwitz, she asked to join us.

So we were three.

The Journey: Mary's Impressions

Sara, Lesley, and I met in Prague and, after several days of touring, flew to Krakow. The next day—August 15, 2004—we hired a car for the 37-mile journey to Auschwitz. It was a lovely summer day, but even the August warmth and the distance of nearly sixty years cannot throw off the chill of Auschwitz. As we drove through the Polish countryside, we witnessed many going to Sunday Mass. Amid the church bells and scenes of families walking or biking to the church, questions filled my head. What had these families been through? After all, some 70,000 Poles died at Auschwitz. Were any of the elderly we saw survivors? What had these Poles suffered in the Nazi occupation (and the subsequent Soviet occupation), and what sort of a mark had the suffering left on ensuing generations? What were their feelings now toward Jews? Were they able to face the antisemitism that has been such a part of the history of Eastern Europe? What sort of sermons would they hear that morning? Would the anti-Jewish teaching that had so long been a part of church teaching be subtly (or not so subtly) woven in, even though such teaching had been repudiated at Vatican II? What difference did it make to these people to participate in Eucharist so close to the town of Oswiecim, which the Nazis had forever changed when they established the horror of Auschwitz?

There was, however, no opportunity to pursue such questions, nor did we talk much en route. Each of us seemed lost in her own world of thought. Once we arrived at Auschwitz I, we were confronted by the stark reality of the camp. We entered the grounds through the infamous gate inscribed with *"Arbeit macht frei"* ("Work makes free"); walked through barracks with various exhibits; went down into the crematorium and gas chamber; placed ourselves in the small starvation cells in Block 11, where four prisoners were forced to stand pressed against each other for days or weeks; and knelt at the Wall of Death where many political prisoners—mostly Poles and Communists—were shot. "Jews weren't worth a bullet to the Nazis," our guide told us.

We then drove to Birkenau (Auschwitz II, about a mile and a half away) to walk the fields where a hundred barracks once housed 100,000 prisoners.[3] Most of Birkenau's buildings no longer remain, as the Nazis destroyed the majority of them prior to the arrival of the Soviet army and took most of the prisoners on a six-thousand-mile death march. The four gas chambers and crematoria, with their capacity to murder and reduce to ashes about 4,400 people daily—mostly Jews—no longer exist, so now the train tracks trail off into the grass. Only a few barracks remain. Yet even in the emptiness we gained some small sense of the unspeakable reality of this extermination center where at least a million Jews were put to death.

Conversing: A Verbal Photograph

After a return to Auschwitz to purchase some books, we drove back to Krakow, where we sat in the Planty, a lovely park near our hotel, and talked for hours—the source of this chapter's title. We have a few notes from our time together, though the typed, linear version each of us now has hardly does justice to the layers of our musings. Even at the time, I think we were all surprised that none of us had cried much. Sara and I had literally wept our way through the United States Holocaust Memorial Museum in Washington, D.C., which we visited together in 1993, and broke down on many occasions while we were at *Yad Vashem*, the Holocaust memorial and education center in Jerusalem, in 1997, especially at the children's memorial. Perhaps it was that no lament can do justice to Auschwitz.

I think of our conversation in the park as a "verbal photograph," which my former teacher Robert McAfee Brown describes as a "moment in time that invests other moments of time with new meaning."[4] I will always remember the three of us, sitting on a bench late on a summer afternoon in the Planty. In that bucolic setting amid families enjoying a pleasant afternoon, we struggled to find words for what we had witnessed. We knew that we could do no more than *begin* to ponder what we had experienced; no amount of conversation could ever add up to "understanding" Auschwitz. But we also knew we needed to be together, not only for the consolation of friendship but also because as Jews and Catholics our remembrance takes on different contours and involves different obligations. We needed to talk across our differences.

A small incident just after we entered the main gate illustrates the distinction. Just a few yards into Auschwitz, Sara was drawn to a plaque in Hebrew, which she began to read aloud. I interpreted this as her way of identifying with the atrocities committed against Jews at Auschwitz, and by extension all the camps.[5] I would not have read it aloud—

"Auschwitz" is properly associated with the genocide of Jews, even though, in fact, most of the Jews died at Birkenau (Auschwitz II), and the vast majority of Poles, Soviet prisoners, Sinti, gays, and lesbians died at Auschwitz I. But more than that, I think Sara instinctively identified with the Jewish prisoners. With whom might I identify? I recoiled from identifying with the Nazis—but would I have been a "bystander," lacking the courage to hide Jews or join the Resistance? I realize now that my preoccupation throughout was the role of the churches, both institutions and individual Christians. To go to Auschwitz as a Christian is to experience deep shame.

Thus, many of my own musings in the park involved trying to "face" the history of my church during the Third Reich and probing implications for the present. Understandably, Sara's reflections went in a different direction.

RUMINATIONS: SARA

Although I have traveled to Israel more than twenty-five times, I never felt a deep need to visit Auschwitz or any other concentration camp sites. So when Mary and I began to discuss the possibility of visiting Auschwitz, I was enthusiastic because I sensed that this would be a unique experience: We were going together, and it was in the larger context of our relationship and work. As a bonus, we were to be joined by Lesley, whom I had come to know and admire for her extraordinary human qualities and passion for justice.

As Mary has reported, the journey from Krakow to Auschwitz was quiet. One of the first things that struck me upon arrival was the presence of so many tour groups and buses. Clearly, relatively few of these people were Jews making a pilgrimage to what has become the symbol of the loss and horrors of the Holocaust. So why were they there? What did this place mean to them? Why, when I discovered a plaque in Hebrew, did I begin to read it aloud? Did I want to say: "Yes, others were killed here, but you should remember what this place meant for the Jewish people and their future?" Perhaps. I also recall that in the crematorium itself we encountered two Israeli couples, and, as they spoke in Hebrew, I wondered what this represented to them as Israelis.

As we talked in that sunny Krakow park, my strongest reaction was anger, not directed toward my Christian colleagues or Christians in general, but against the brutality of the Nazis who thought Jews were not worth a bullet. I felt outrage at those who had destroyed all the children, like my own, who were the Jewish future, and who deliberately created conditions that dehumanized people solely because they were Jews. I came to understand that perhaps instantaneous and unexpected death was preferable to the conditions under which Jewish prisoners had to live, which we saw for ourselves at Birkenau.

In the crematorium, there was a single *Yahrzeit* candle.[6] It reminded me that in the children's memorial at *Yad Vashem* there is a single candle reflected so many times by mirrors that it appears to be thousands of candles. The Midrash (Jewish commentary) teaches us that if you save one life you save a world, and if you destroy a life you destroy a world. My realization was that the sin of the Nazis was not only against those they tortured and killed, but also against the whole Jewish people and, therefore, against me personally.

At the same time, the opportunity for the three of us to reflect together afterward was an important corrective to my seeing Auschwitz and what it implies as a solely Jewish phenomenon. They rightly reminded me about the others who died there and about the genocides that continue in our world—Cambodia, Rwanda, Srebrenica, Darfur—where people are massacred just because of who they are. On the other hand, I explained how the psyche of Jews is infused with the memory of the Holocaust and how it leads to a mentality of "never again." We as Jews firmly believe that in the face of danger, our inaction and that of others might lead to what happened in the Holocaust. This plays out strongly in the significance of Israel as a sovereign state, enjoined not only to use its power to protect its citizens but also to save Jews elsewhere in the world from harm, including by rescue.

The experience of the Holocaust affects Jewish sovereignty and power embodied in the State of Israel. While in Jerusalem in February 2005 at a seminar in honor of those of us who had just received the President's Award for Distinguished Leadership of Jewish Education in the Diaspora, I responded to a speech by Professor Ruth Gavison of Hebrew University. She argued that Israel is unique in that, *as a Jewish state*, it must make decisions about the use of force or combat to respond to perceived danger to its citizens. We, as Jews in the United States, do not make such decisions. They are made by the government, whether we agree or not.

In the presence of Mary and Lesley, I felt compelled to make clear why Jews resent universalizing the Holocaust, that is, using the term generically to apply to other tragic situations. I thought about the sheer numbers (six million Jews), about how many great scholars and potentially great scholars had been lost, and about the children. Had, for example, the brilliant scholar Rabbi Abraham Joshua Heschel not been rescued, he would have been gassed. The world would have been so much poorer without his extraordinary humanity and learning. We will never know how many great scholars and potential scholars the Nazis killed, nor will we know how many religious and civic leaders they put to death in the most degrading ways. While not minimizing the cruelty that continues in the world, we must never lose sight of the particularity of the Shoah.

Nevertheless, I continue to feel cautious about making the Holocaust a central foundation for Jewish identity. Jewish identity must be founded on Jewish practices and texts, not on victimization. So it is vital that Jewish education provide a firm grounding in Judaica. I also came away from Auschwitz-Birkenau with a renewed conviction about how important it is for Jews to wrestle with what happened there and how it has shaped our psyches. It was at Auschwitz-Birkenau that I confronted anew my anger at our loss, which renewed my conviction that we must do everything possible to build strong and compelling communities of Jews everywhere in the world. In such communities, Jews can come to experience the power of Judaism, not just resolve to keep Judaism alive as a response to the Holocaust.

I ponder how my visit with two deeply religious Catholic women was different from one I might have made with fellow Jews. Because of my work with Mary over many years, in some respects I had already confronted the issue of the anti-Jewish teachings of Christianity that prepared fertile ground for Germany's National Socialism. I had explored the controversy over the role of Pope Pius XII and the complicity of the churches, so these questions did not preoccupy me as they did Mary. In retrospect, being in their company seems to have made it possible for me to express my anger without concluding that Christianity is inherently anti-Jewish. What I did take away from our experience is the firm conviction that if we are to create a better world, we will have to do it together as Jews and Christians.

RUMINATIONS: MARY

The sixtieth anniversary of the liberation of Auschwitz by Soviet troops from the Ukraine on January 27, 1945, occurred as I began drafting this chapter. News stories reported about leaders from more than forty nations, survivors, and Jewish and Christian officials who gathered first in Krakow and then in Auschwitz to commemorate the anniversary. The guest list also included at least three of the liberators, one of whom, Genry Koptev Gomolov, told a reporter that when they entered the camp:

> He and his comrades found thousands of wraithlike people laughing and crying, singing and shouting, or simply staring dumbly at their liberators. He saw corpses stacked like cordwood and abandoned before the Nazis could set them on fire. He saw the crematories and the subterranean rooms he later learned were gas chambers.[7]

At the time, Gomolov was an eighteen-year-old Pole drafted into the Red Army. It staggers the imagination to consider what he and his fellow soldiers must have experienced as they encountered some 600 emaciated prisoners at the slave labor camp of Auschwitz I, and another 5,800 at the larger compound of Birkenau (or Auschwitz II). The world today is familiar with photos and film clips of those skeletal victims, but no visual representation can begin to account for the culture of terror that reigned in the camps. As horrifying as the term *genocide* is, it fails to convey the particulars: inmates half-frozen in the bitter cold of the Polish winter, soiled and malodorous from the degrading conditions, deadened in body and spirit. Nor can our visit in August 2004 convey the desolation of sixty years ago. In a speech given at the dinner preceding the Auschwitz commemoration, Moshe Kantor, chairman of the European Jewish Congress, recounted meeting an elderly woman while visiting Birkenau several years ago. She remarked on how different the camp looked from when she had been interned. Then there was no grass. The starving prisoners had eaten it all.[8]

The particulars: These draw me in and force me to dwell in the concrete world of the victims, albeit at a safe remove of some sixty years. Sometimes I am surprised by what has been most memorable. When Sara and I had visited the United States Holocaust Memorial Museum, I had been especially moved by the exhibit with the shoes—mounds of victims' shoes, piled high. While I am unsure of the precise reason that particular exhibit touched me so deeply, I suspect it may be that items as commonplace as shoes remind us that ordinary people from all walks of life were taken from everything that was familiar and placed in a hell fashioned by human hands. Shoes remind us, as historian Yaffa Eliach says, that "there was once a world."[9]

Auschwitz also has shoes: 43,525 pairs of prisoners' shoes, to be exact. It is also the place where a prisoner deprived of food for more than a week in the starvation cell of Block 11 ate his own shoes.[10] In the section of Birkenau called "Canada," the liberators discovered, in addition to the shoes, 13,964 carpets, 69,848 dishes, 348,820 men's suits, and 836,255 women's garments. Many of these are now displayed in the barracks of Auschwitz I, along with other artifacts of Nazi plunder: enormous piles of glasses, false teeth, toothbrushes and shaving brushes, collections of *tallitot* (prayer shawls)—and seven tons of human hair.[11] The Nazis intended to waste nothing to promote the war effort, though, in fact, the camp guards ransacked much for their own purposes.[12]

Shoes, eyeglasses, hair, clothes, and suitcases, many with their owner's name inscribed, remain as remnants of people regarded as "vermin," as "expendables." Then other particulars: numbers. I was struck by the sheer size and scale of the camps. More than 100,000 prisoners were crammed into the filth of the Birkenau barracks. At least 1.1 million men, women, and children were exterminated there.

The statistics are staggering, overwhelming—and abstract. But the artifacts are concrete. They not only bear witness that "there was once a world," but they also pose a question: How could this world have been nearly destroyed in "civilized"

Europe in the twentieth century? Even if I were a scholar of the Holocaust, I could not answer that question to anyone's satisfaction. But the complexity of the question does not excuse me from grappling with it, because "my people"—Catholics— have particular reasons that we "cannot pass by the tragedy of the Shoah": We are implicated.

I can do justice in this chapter neither to the full ramifications of that indictment nor to the probing work of historians, theologians, and ethicists, including Catholic thinkers, on the Holocaust. Rather, my purpose is to continue briefly that conversation in the Krakow Planty by taking up a question that Sara and I posed to participants in the Catholic-Jewish Colloquium that we directed from 1993 to 1995.[13] After an evening spent discussing the Holocaust in our fourth gathering with the participants in January 1994, we asked them: "What impact does the Holocaust have on relations between Jews and Catholics today?" It was, as we remarked in chapter 4, a difficult discussion. Perhaps it required a prior question: "What are the particular issues Catholics have to ask themselves when they confront Auschwitz?"

In addressing what Catholics need to consider, several things stand out. One is the necessity of attending to the particulars of history. We need to analyze the factors that enabled so many in the German Catholic Church to acquiesce to Hitler—and that account for relatively few Catholics throughout Europe, including church leaders, having resisted the Nazis. As historian Michael Phayer documents, European Catholic attitudes toward Jews before the Holocaust varied considerably from country to country. Although all inherited the long legacy of anti-Judaism—theological disparagement of Judaism—in some countries, notably, Poland, Croatia, Hungary, Slovakia, and Austria, a deeper contempt for Jews had taken root. Some church leaders professed admiration of Hitler, such as Austrian Bishop Alois Hudal, later the rector of the German College in Rome. The priest-president of Slovakia, Josef Tiso, was complicit in the passage of anti-Semitic legislation and ultimately in the genocide of Slovakian Jews. Yet under the leadership of German bishop Konrad Graf von Preysing, Margarete Sommer established an organization that rescued many Jews in Berlin and tried, unsuccessfully, to have the German episcopacy and Pope Pius XII speak out against Nazism.[14]

In Germany itself, the *Kulturkampf* of Otto von Bismarck in the 1870s had meant that many German Catholics perceived themselves as an embattled minority, despite their near-equality in numbers to Protestants. As a consequence, they developed an intense patriotism that intensified after World War I into a sort of hyper-nationalism. Moreover, in the months prior to the Concordat (*Reichskonkordat*) of 1933, in which the Nazis agreed to guarantee the Catholic Church the freedom to practice its faith, Nazis had harassed many church members and organizations.

When we look to the theological stances of church leaders in Germany in the 1930s and 1940s, we see the profound consequence of the view articulated at the First Vatican Council (1869–1870) that the church is a "perfect society" distinct from and superior to other human societies. For many German bishops and theologians, this understanding of the church—an ecclesiology—entailed a desire to restore medieval Christendom and thus to reject modernity, with its emphasis on liberal thought, democracy, and the secular state. Those who saw the church as a perfect society looked askance at the parliamentary democracy established in the post–World War I Weimar Republic. Hitler's dictatorship seemed to offer a better possibility.

Perhaps the most dangerous aspect of this theological perspective was the belief that the church's primary mission was the *spiritual* good of its members. Thus, the hierarchy was reluctant to challenge Hitler, lest he close the churches. In their view, "as long as the churches were operating, the pope and bishops were fulfilling their duty of making God's grace available to the faithful."[15] The German bishops and the Vatican were critical of some aspects of Nazi belief, like its neo-paganism, and certain actions, such as the suppression of Catholic organizations. But as a body they voiced no objection to the national boycott of Jewish businesses and the dismissal of Jews from positions of civil service in April 1933. They offered no public outcry when the Nuremberg Laws were passed in 1935, and no official protest after *Kristallnacht*, that tragic night of the "shattered glass" (November 9–10, 1938) during which Nazis destroyed 267 synagogues, murdered 91 Jews, desecrated Jewish cemeteries, and sent more than 20,000 Jews to concentration camps.[16]

Some Catholic leaders spoke out consistently against the Nazis, including Bishop (later Cardinal) Konrad Graf von Preysing of Berlin and Bishop Johannes Baptist Sproll of Rottenburg, as well as theologians Romano Guardini and Engelbert Krebs. Many others, while mindful of the threat to the church that National Socialism posed, nevertheless regarded the rule of Hitler to be preferable to modern democratic regimes—and certainly to Bolshevism.

Among many insights Robert Krieg proffers about this period, two seem especially pertinent. The first has to do with an assumption that set Guardini and Krebs apart from their theological colleagues who were more approving of the Third Reich: The latter group adhered to a narrative of the West as having degenerated since the Middle Ages; therefore, they sought a leader who would restore Christendom. Guardini and Krebs, in contrast, engaged in a critical dialogue with modernity, affirming the importance of human rights and democracy. Krieg's concluding section about the inadequacy of ecclesiology during the Nazi era is particularly relevant. Church officials had cast suspicion on a number of twentieth-century theologians who had departed from the categories of neo-

Scholasticism and had grappled seriously with modernity. And too many theologians themselves had failed to learn from the social sciences and move outside their narrow frameworks:

> [F]or a century, the papacy and episcopacy had stifled scholars' intellectual freedom, thereby preventing them from critically reflecting on the character of modernity and on the church's nature and mission in the contemporary world.... [T]he majority of theologians during the 1920s and 1930s ... conceiving of the church as a medieval fortress or a Gothic cathedral under siege from liberalism and secularism ... failed to recognize the valid insights of modern thought and the constructive elements of a parliamentary democracy.[17]

Beyond the dynamics of individual nations is the role of Pope Pius XII. Some have made him *the* preeminent symbol of the failure of Christianity during the Shoah, the one religious figure whom later generations can evoke as representing the hollowness of Christian morality. This demonization has elicited an emotional defense by many Catholics, who support him as a hero. Lacking the credentials of a historian and the access to primary documents, I can only say that in my reading, Pius XII should neither be demonized nor canonized. Rather, he played the role of cautious diplomat when the world needed a prophet. His neutrality in the face of the unspeakable evil of the Shoah reveals how little the lives of Jews meant in the face of ostensibly preserving the welfare of the Catholic Church.

In his highly regarded book *Pius XII and the Holocaust*, historian José M. Sánchez analyzes possible reasons that the pope did not speak out more forthrightly against the Nazi regime. In his judgment, a number of charges that various historians have leveled against Pius XII lack substance, such as the claim that he was an anti-Semite, that he feared primarily for the destruction of Rome and the security of the Vatican, that he feared Soviet Communism more than German Nazism, and that his admiration for German culture muted his criticism of the Nazi government.

Sanchez cites five principal reasons that in his view account for why Pius XII did not speak forthrightly against the Third Reich: (1) his fear that a protest would instigate the Nazis to abrogate the Concordat of 1933, thus leaving German Catholics open to persecution; (2) his training as a diplomat, combined with a personal predilection for prudence; (3) his reluctance to create a crisis of conscience for German Catholics in which they had to choose between a powerful, authoritarian state and their faith; (4) his desire to remain neutral so that he could serve to mediate an end to the war; and (5) his fear of making the situation worse. Sánchez maintains that this final reason is the strongest; Pius told people both in private and in public that quiet diplomacy and private action would save more lives than public protest.

But, many ask, how could his action have made things any worse? This, however, is a question asked in retrospect, when we know so much about the way in which plans developed for the Final Solution. As Sánchez asks, did Pius XII know that the Germans sought to eliminate all Jews—and if he knew of it, did he believe it possible, even comprehensible?[18]

Papal power being finite—much more so than it may appear to outsiders—Pius XII could neither have prevented nor ended the Nazi madness. Nevertheless, his reluctance to embolden action by church leaders and to stand as a symbol of resistance to Hitler not only contributed to the tragedy of the Shoah, but also undermined the moral suasion of the papacy, and indeed the entire church, for years to come. Much later (1975), the synod of dioceses in the then-Federal Republic of Germany would confess:

> [W]e were, nevertheless, as a whole, a church commu-
> nity who kept on living our lives while turning our
> backs too often on the fate of this persecuted Jewish
> people. We looked too fixedly at the threat to our own
> institutions and remained silent about the crimes com-
> mitted against the Jews and Judaism.[19]

Larger forces were at work as well. The excesses of the
Enlightenment had left many European Catholics suspicious of
modernism and revolutionary change. Many tended to conflate
democracy, liberalism, secularism, and atheism. Added to this
was a fear of Bolshevism. Indeed, the atheism of Communism
seemed a greater threat to some than the fascism of the Nazis.
As John Pawlikowski has pointed out, at that time the Catholic
Church lacked a theory of human rights. He argues that "at the
level of institutional Christianity fear of liberalism and concern
for the loss of the church's influence over the public order were
in fact stronger motives for acquiescence or even collaboration
with Nazism and Fascism than classical Christian antisemitism
itself." Pawlikowski asks whether the church might have
responded differently if it had heeded those who advocated a
more liberal perspective, including attention to human rights.
Moreover, he speculates that had church leaders established a
working relationship with liberal opposition to the Third
Reich, such as that forged within the "Zegota" movement in
Poland between Catholic lay leaders and people whose social
ideology had an anti-religious but pro-humanist bent, more
Jews, especially children, would have been rescued.[20]

Perhaps the greatest challenge we Catholics have is to let
the Holocaust "interrupt" us—that is, to challenge longstanding ways of thinking about Christianity, to "interrogate" our
religious identity. "Ask yourselves," Johann-Baptist Metz says,
"if the theology you are learning is such that it could remain
unchanged before and after Auschwitz. If this be the case, be

on your guard."[21] This imperative from Metz is widely cited, and many theologians take it seriously.

Yet on the level of everyday church life, it seems we have barely begun to face the church's complicity for Auschwitz. Aside from the occasional mention at a Sunday Eucharist prior to *Yom HaShoah* (Holocaust Remembrance Day in the Jewish calendar), I cannot recall an occasion when "Auschwitz" in any way figured in preaching. It is significant that the diocese of Naples, Florida, sponsors an annual *Yom HaShoah* service. But the challenge is to integrate what that service means for Christian life today. Similarly, it is important that the curriculum of many Catholic schools includes teaching about the Holocaust and that Seton Hill University sponsors the National Catholic Center for Holocaust Education. It is not enough, however, to learn *about* the Shoah: It is incumbent on Catholics to ponder its implications for church life today.

One implication for Catholics from study of the Shoah is that our history is always on the table with Jews. We have to grapple with the terrible things done in the name of Christ. We have to respect Sara's anger: Jews have a right to be angry. Auschwitz indicts the church. We must not turn away from the indictment defensively. Rather, in facing our history, we engage in a real act of asceticism.

Lest the notion of "facing history" seem a bit on the abstract side, our traveling companion, Lesley, taught me a lesson in its concrete application. Having lived and worked with impoverished people, especially children, in Winnipeg, Manitoba, virtually her entire professional life, she was in the process of opening a Catholic Worker House immediately after our return from Auschwitz. On the plane en route home, she said that the encounter with the utter degradation that the Nazis forced upon their prisoners had helped her resolve a policy question. She would see to it that one of the lavatories of the Catholic Worker House be available to street people.

Everyone, she said, has the right to take care of basic human needs in a manner that respects their dignity as persons.

What, then, does Auschwitz mean for the relationship between Jews and Christians? I return to Clark Williamson's assertion: "Conversation with Jews is indispensable to understanding Christian faith ... the historical evidence massively attests to the fact that apart from listening and talking with Jews, we will misunderstand the Christian faith and act on our misunderstandings."[22] Conversation, however, rests on trust—and history, most especially what Auschwitz represents, provides many reasons for Jews not to trust Christians. To be a genuine conversation partner means to live in such a way as to be trustworthy.

One way of earning this trust is to learn about Jewish life—the life before the Nazi genocide and the life of Jews today. We must never reduce our knowledge of Judaism to knowledge of the Holocaust, nor think of Jews primarily as victims. If we are able to have a better sense of Jewish learning, culture, and practice, we will be better able to appreciate the profundity of Judaism and its importance to the world, and less inclined to view it from a position of religious superiority. Finally, we Christians pray as Jesus taught us, "Deliver us from evil." Confrontation with the Shoah teaches us that this deliverance must include active resistance to evil, lest we be complicit in the creation and maintenance of other places that could rightly be described as "hell on earth."

A CONVERSATION CONTINUED: SARA

The pilgrimage of a Jew to Auschwitz not only thrusts one into the horrible realities that Auschwitz represents but also into the profound and disturbing questions that Jews must confront in the wake of the Holocaust. As Rabbi Jonathan Sacks writes:

> If we were to incorporate the Shoah into the narrative
> of Jewish history, as just one more chapter in the
> chronicle of exiles, destructions, inquisitions, and
> pogroms of the past, we would be hiding from the sin-
> gularity that made this experience like no other. The
> traditional hermeneutic of Jewish self-understanding
> is "ruptured."[23]

The singularity of the Shoah as event, phenomenon, and
tragedy is unparalleled in Jewish history and probably in
human experience. The Holocaust looms over our time. It is no
surprise, then, that the course on the Holocaust has had the
largest single registration over the past two decades in the
undergraduate program offered by Hebrew Union College at
the University of Southern California; the students are both
Jews and non-Jews. The many Holocaust memorials and museums in the United States and beyond our shores testify to the
powerful hold the Holocaust has on the minds and hearts of
Jews. They also reflect our passion that the rest of the world
learn the depth of this genocide and the lessons it carries about
the dangers of hate and racism. Moreover, sites such as the
United States Holocaust Memorial Museum in Washington,
D.C., and *Yad Vashem* in Jerusalem confront the visitor with
the hard evidence of the devastation, lest any credence be given
to Holocaust "deniers."[24] The mounds of shoes, suitcases,
human hair, and clothes bear witness in a visceral way.

Yet these memorials and museums are of more recent vin-
tage. In the immediate aftermath of the Holocaust, public discussion was sparse. Despite the knowledge available through
documents, witnesses, and survivors, there seemed to be such a
shock that silence prevailed. Many survivors themselves
refused to speak about what they had experienced. As the veil
of silence began to lift, however, among the first issues raised
were profound questions about the apparent absence of God,

the enduring nature of the covenant between God and the Jewish people, and the place of the Holocaust in the historical narrative of the Jewish people.

When Richard Rubinstein asked in 1966, "How can Jews believe in an omnipotent, beneficent God after Auschwitz?" he raised what would become the central question for Jewish theologians.[25] We might wonder about the importance of such a question for many Jews who either do not accept God as an actor in human history or even doubt the existence of a transcendent God. Yet, as Michael Rosenak argues, five fundamental ideas stand at the center of classical Jewish literature: the God of Israel, the Torah of Israel, the people of Israel, the Land of Israel, and the Messiah.[26] For Rosenak, every Jewish theology or ideology has to deal with these ideas and their interrelationships, even as new challenges that emerge internally or externally affect their understanding. Thus, the questions about God that emerge from the Holocaust go to the very heart of any contemporary Jewish theology or ideology.

I do not intend to review here the many reconstructions of Jewish theology spawned by a question such as Rubinstein's, but rather to direct readers to some of the important thinkers whose works I find compelling. I am thinking primarily of Eliezer Berkovits, Emil Fackenhiem, and Irving Greenberg.[27] Yet Jewish thought varies widely:

> For the religious believer, the Holocaust confirms his faith; for the unbeliever it confirms his lack of faith. For the radical it creates a novum in history; for the traditionalist it recalls earlier catastrophes. For the pietist it testifies to God's suffering presence in the world; for the secularist it proves His absence. These variant readings have shown no tendency to converge over time.[28]

The sheer complexity of the theological and ideological questions that emerge from the Holocaust challenges all those charged with educating Jews and guiding Jewish communities to be aware of their own biases. Furthermore, we must ask ourselves how we are to talk about God, the covenant, and the historic destiny of the Jewish people in a manner that gives credence to the issues raised by the Holocaust, but does not overwhelm the wisdom, beauty, and gifts that the Jewish tradition has offered us over the centuries. This brings me back to the question I brought with me to Auschwitz and which continues to occupy not only my thinking but also that of others: In what ways should the Holocaust—the questions it raises and the emotional hold it has on Jews, regardless of their ideology—become the raw material with which we try to build Jewish identity in the face of ongoing assimilation, conflicts within our community, and a decline in Jewish knowledge and practice? As compelling as the Holocaust is in its very tragedy, it can play too great a role in Jewish identity.

The Holocaust as destruction and the State of Israel as rebirth are often linked. As Irving Greenberg says, "The reborn State of Israel is the fundamental act of life and meaning after Auschwitz. To fail to grasp that inextricable connection and response is to fail to comprehend the theological significance of Israel."[29] The March of the Living, a two-week intensive experience where Jewish adolescents travel to Poland (including Auschwitz) and Israel for a highly structured educational experience, is apparently successful in inspiring Jewish adolescents about their own Jewish identity.[30] Yet I question how this kind of emotional connection translates into the ongoing life of young Jews in their home communities. This is the challenge we face: to be true to the Holocaust and the questions it raises for traditional understandings of God, covenant, and the mission of the Jewish people, while connecting Jews to the enduring values that have sustained us over the centuries and are the building blocks of Jewish identity in the contemporary world.

My involvement in the world of interreligious learning over these past twenty years has made clear how problematic the Holocaust is in any Jewish-Christian engagement. The issue is so much in the forefront that the Jewish scholars who wrote "*Dabru Emet*: A Statement on Christians and Christianity," included a section on Nazism and Christianity: "Without the long history of Christian anti-Judaism and Christian violence against Jews, Nazi ideology could not have taken hold nor could it have been carried out." Yet they continue: "But Nazism itself was not an inevitable outcome of Christianity." The title of this section—Nazism was not a Christian phenomenon—elicited criticism from Jewish leaders as well as from Christian scholars as essentially "letting Christians and Christianity off the hook."[31]

Beyond official statements, however, are the real-life feelings of Jews and Christians on the matter of the Holocaust. In the Catholic-Jewish Colloquium, which we described in chapter 4, the painful reality, even among individuals who became colleagues and friends, was the sense that Jews came to the discussion as victims and Christians as possible perpetrators. Whatever the intellectual engagement around the issues of the Holocaust, it is the emotional loadings of anxiety, shame, guilt, awkwardness, and anger that are always present. There is probably no way to dismiss these emotions, as Mary has discussed in her reflections.

Our visit to the United States Holocaust Memorial Museum in 1993 and our journey to Auschwitz in 2004 were important in allowing us to share honestly the emotions that the Holocaust engenders in both of us and to process those emotions in the presence of each other. There are probably too few encounters that would afford Christians and Jews that same kind of experience. Such an experience needs to be built on a solid foundation of trust and empathy. While not mitigating the importance of sharing the emotional loadings that Jews and Christians bring to the conversation, confronting the meanings that might be drawn from the Holocaust about the future for Christian-Jewish relations is an essential task.

Both Christian and Jewish scholars have attempted to draw lessons from the Holocaust as to how Jews and Christians might build anew their relationship to one another and together create a better future for the societies in which they live.[32] At the heart of things is the necessity for a renewed commitment to work together for justice for all people, to eradicate hatred and racism, and to ensure the health and welfare of all citizens of the world. Although the commitments have been made, we cannot be very pleased with the achievements thus far. Hatred, poverty, hunger, inhumane treatment of people, genocide, and war are still with us and show little signs of diminishing. In the end, then, what might we learn from the Holocaust that would help us understand how we need to relate to each other? Although there have been many Christians who have concerned themselves with these questions, I turn, in particular, to some lessons from a Jewish perspective.

Rabbi Irving Greenberg has drawn compelling and challenging insights from the Holocaust as they apply to Jews and Christians. He notes, "The Holocaust suggests a fundamental skepticism about all human movements, left and right, political and religious—even as we participate in them. Nothing dare evoke our absolute, unquestioning loyalty, not even our God."[33] Such a statement sounds shocking at first glance. If we are not to have absolute, unquestioning loyalty to God, what kind of relationship should we have? Is our model Abraham at Sodom and Gomorrah (Gen. 18:20–33), where God's justice is called into question? Or is our model the obedient Abraham responding to God's call to sacrifice his son, Isaac (Gen. 22:1–18)?

How do we know when to question? What should be our moral compass? Greenberg believes that one of the lessons we should learn from the Holocaust is the danger of absolutism. There is great danger in any belief system that extends its finite understanding, limited by our humanness, to an infinite claim, which is essentially the province of the Divine. He labels such a claim idolatry.[34] In turn, Greenberg's criticism of absolutism leads him to advocate a theology of religious pluralism:

> Pluralism is made possible by the ability of a religion or a truth system to maintain its vitality and to continue to move its adherents even in the presence of the other.... The pluralist affirms the absolute values but has come to know their limits. They do not cover all the possibilities. Pluralism is an absolutism that has come to recognize its own limitations.[35]

If Christians and Jews were to make this understanding a fundamental principle of how to interact with each other and the message they wish to give the world, we will have learned an important lesson from the Holocaust.

Perhaps it is ironic that the tragedy of the Holocaust compels us to recognize our human limitations. The Nazi atrocities, emerging from a nation of highly educated and rational citizens, warn us that human beings, no matter how highly cultured, are capable of unspeakable evils. They warn us of the dangers of an absolute ideology that overwhelmed the humanistic values developed over centuries. Silence in the presence of these atrocities demonstrates that even people of religious faith can be deterred from moral action in the presence of absolute power.

It is this recognition of human limitations that provides the foundation for true encounter between Christians and Jews. The recognition that we cannot fully know the mystery of God means we are all seekers of religious truth, each in our own way. We can learn from one another, appreciate the beauty of one another's tradition, and challenge one another.

Where is the irony in all this for a Jew? After Auschwitz, the first reaction a Jew might have is withdrawal and the erection of a barrier of suspicion about all non-Jews. Indeed, many have done just that. Encountering Auschwitz with Mary and Lesley, serious Catholics, and reflecting upon that experience leads me in the opposite direction. As Jews, we have an obligation to join with people of religious faith to ensure that religious belief knows its limitations and that religious faith is dedicated to the highest ideals of social justice for all humanity. This will be possible only if we learn together the ways in which we are all partners in *tikkun olam*, the repair of the world. And only when Christians and Jews face Auschwitz in one another's presence will reconciliation be possible.

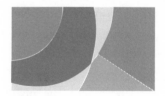

7

JEWS, CHRISTIANS, AND THE LAND OF ISRAEL

In January 1997, Sara and I entered the El Al terminal at New York's John F. Kennedy Airport to fly to Israel, where we would meet Dorothy Bass the next day. Because we are both obsessive about time, we arrived several hours before our flight, particularly because we know that El Al's security arrangements are the most stringent of all airlines. We were not prepared, however, for the interrogation we received.

When we entered the ticketing area, we were the only two passengers. Although it was obvious we were traveling together, agents separated us so that a different person questioned each of us about the purpose and itinerary of our trip. What soon emerged as a major stumbling block was that a Jew and a Christian were traveling together. Each of us told her interrogator, a young Israeli, that we had worked together in Jewish-Christian relations for many years and that we wanted to share our different perspectives on Israel with one another, as well as with the Protestant minister who would join us.

What proof did we have of our collaboration? Fortunately, I had with me several copies of the issue of *Religious Education* that we had jointly edited, and I showed that to my agent, who seemed unimpressed. He then asked me to verify my employment at Union Theological Seminary. As I had only my business card, having left what I thought were nonessential identification cards at home, this deepened his suspicions— after all, anyone could have such a card printed. Even more suspect, I had a new passport, as my previous ones, carrying the imprint of six previous trips to Israel, had expired.

Then my interrogator changed places with Sara's, and the questioning began all over again—only she was now being questioned in Hebrew. At least her passport indicated the frequency of her trips to Israel. Just when we thought the two agents were finished, they left but asked us to remain. Then their supervisor appeared and once again we went through the cycle of the same questions. Although by this time—our interrogation lasted forty-five minutes—other passengers must have begun to line up, I have no memory of any scene other than that of the two of us before the incredulous agents.

They finally let us proceed, but we never knew the reasons for their skepticism. Perhaps they were secular Israelis, who, lacking knowledge of the rapprochement between Jews and Christians in our time, simply could not imagine our having a collegial relationship. We thought it improbable that we matched any security tips El Al might have had, as we seemed an unlikely pair to engage in terrorism.

In retrospect, this incident serves as a parable about the emotionally charged issue of Israel in the Jewish-Christian relationship. So many of the complexities of this relationship are at play whenever Israel is in the picture. Israel, after all, is the *site* of the historical development of both our religious traditions, a *symbol* each tradition interprets in varying ways, a *symptom* of religious conflict, and a *sacred* land in a *secular state*.

Just as scripture, sacred for both Jews and Christians, is understood differently and thereby both unites and divides, so too does Israel. As in the previous chapter, we will alternate in addressing this claim.

ISRAEL IN THE JEWISH TRADITION: SARA

For Jews throughout history, the Land of Israel, *Eretz Yisrael,* is central to understanding Judaism and the mission and destiny of the Jewish people. Jews regard the Land of Israel as *Moledet,* their homeland as a people, just as Christians regard it as the birthplace of Jesus and the church.

Muslim tradition teaches that the Prophet Muhammad (570–632) had visited Jerusalem, brought there in a mysterious manner by the hand of God. Thus, Muslims came to regard Jerusalem as a holy city, a spiritual center of their monotheistic predecessors. So Jerusalem is a city sacred to three monotheistic religions. Yet, too often, Jerusalem has become a site of violence and bloodshed, as competing religious traditions struggled with each other.

Today, Jerusalem is the capital of the State of Israel. Alongside its modern, bustling streets and buildings on the western side of the city stands the Old City, filled with holy places for Christians, Jews, and Muslims, where echoes of past struggles and present tensions reverberate. There can be no indepth conversation between Christians and Jews that does not confront the meanings of *Eretz Yisrael* and Holy Land for our respective communities. The creation of the State of Israel in 1948 has been both a cause for celebration by Christians and Jews and a reality that has provoked misunderstanding and friction between our two communities.

So it seemed important for us to go to Israel together if we were to confront the challenges this land poses for interreligious learning. Of course, Mary and I had each been to Israel many times before our joint trip in 1997. Members of the

Catholic-Jewish Colloquium had urged us to create an interreligious learning experience for them in Israel, but we had never
succeeded in finding the funding necessary to support such a
trip. Nevertheless, we thought their understanding of the
importance of such an encounter was compelling enough for us
to undertake the journey together.

Our Protestant colleague, Dr. Dorothy Bass, who had
sponsored some of our earlier projects as the director of the
Valparaiso Project on the Education and Formation of People
in Faith, decided to join us because she had never been to
Israel. So we set off to share a journey that evoked many of our
deepest sensibilities and stimulated lively conversations. Our
itinerary was in part shaped by Jewish perspectives on the
Land of Israel.

For Jews, the attachment to the land goes back to the
promise by God to Abram in Genesis 12:7: "The Lord
appeared to Abram and said, 'I will assign this land to your offspring.' And he built an altar there to the Lord who had
appeared to him." This promise is repeated many times to the
descendants of Abram and becomes central to the development
of the Hebrews as they evolved from a desert tribe to the
People Israel. The Exodus from Egypt and the journey of forty
years through the desert to the Promised Land is the fundamental narrative of the Jewish people. The sojourn of
Abraham in Egypt, the enslavement of the Hebrews in Egypt,
and all the other incidents of separation from the land became
paradigmatic of the themes of exile and redemption that permeate Jewish history. Arnold Eisen, a scholar of Jewish philosophy, devotes an entire book to the relationship between
homelessness and return as they are woven throughout Jewish
history and thought.[1]

For Jews, return to the land and ultimate redemption are
inextricably tied together. Neither the destruction of the
Temple of Solomon and exile to Babylonia in 586 B.C.E. nor the

destruction of the Second Temple in 70 C.E. permanently severed the tie of Jews to *Eretz Yisrael*. In fact, in the nearly two thousand years of dispersion prior to the establishment of the State of Israel in 1948, *Eretz Yisrael* was never far from the consciousness of most Jews, no matter where they lived.

Jews face east to Jerusalem when we pray. In the core of Jewish liturgy, the *Amidah*, three of the eighteen blessings refer to the Land of Israel (Zion) and Jerusalem:

- Gather the dispersed from the ends of the earth. Blessed are You, Lord, who gathers the dispersed of His People Israel.

- Have mercy, O Lord, and return to Jerusalem, Your city. Dwell there as You promised and build it now, in our days for all time. Reestablish quickly there the throne of David, Your servant. Blessed are You, Lord, who builds Jerusalem.

- May we witness Your merciful return to Zion. Blessed are You, Lord, who restores His Presence to Jerusalem.

Barry Holtz captures the way in which the liturgical cycle connects Jews who live far from *Eretz Yisrael* to the actual geography and reality of the land:

> The traditional liturgy changes the wording of the service to reflect the seasonal cycle of *Eretz Yisrael*, praying for rain in the winter and dew in the summer. Indeed, special liturgical poems are recited twice a year to mark the point in the season that these daily prayers are changed. Prayers for rain and dew ... essentially move the worshipper out of his or her own specific geographical locality into another place—the Land of Israel, *not* as symbol or ideal, but as a living reality, a place where actual fruits grow, where dew or rain falls

in a seasonal routine different from that which most of
us experience in North America.[2]

Beyond liturgy, connections to *Eretz Yisrael* are woven into the
life-cycle rituals, the festivals of the Jewish year, and the blessings
we recite on an everyday basis. In the Jewish marriage ceremony,
the presider recites seven blessing, of which two explicitly
include Jerusalem and Zion. The traditional blessing after meals,
Birkat HaMazon, also refers to Zion and Jerusalem. Jewish tradition calls three of the major festivals of the year "pilgrimage"
festivals, because on those occasions Jews from all over the Land
of Israel brought offerings to the Temple in Jerusalem. These festivals—Sukkot, Pesach, and Shavuot—are connected to the agricultural cycle in the Land of Israel, as well as to historic events
in the life of the Jewish people. At the end of the Passover Seder
we recite, "To next year in Jerusalem." Even in death the Land
of Israel is part of the ritual. It is traditional for Jews to be buried
with a small sack of earth from *Eretz Yisrael*. Some Jews request
burial in Israel itself.

The texts that Jews hold sacred, starting with the Bible,
are suffused with references to Israel as the "Promised Land"
for the Jewish people, a land unique in its qualities and a land
that is to be regarded as home. The Passover Haggadah that
frames the ritual of the Passover Seder was created over time
by rabbinic scholars. Today, there are many and varied
Passover Haggadot, reflecting a diversity of interests and
views among contemporary Jews. In each, however, the telling
of the Exodus narrative begins with the following verses from
Deuteronomy:

A wandering Aramean was my father, and he went
down into Egypt, and sojourned there, few in number;
and he became there a great nation, great, mighty, and
populous. And the Egyptians dealt ill with us, and

afflicted us, and laid upon us hard bondage. And we cried unto the Lord, the God of our fathers, and the Lord heard our voice, and saw our affliction, and our toil, and our oppression. And the Lord brought us forth out of Egypt with a mighty hand, and with an out-stretched arm, and with great terribleness, and with signs, and with wonders. And He hath brought us into this place, and hath given us this land, a land flowing with milk and honey. (Deut. 26: 5–19)

Although the Exodus from Egypt is the fundamental narrative of the Jewish people, it is always tied to the ultimate goal, settlement in the Land of Israel in order to carry out God's commandments and to advance, as the Jewish people, God's mission for the world and humanity. From the Torah through the rabbinic texts and all the commentaries until the present, Jews have heard this message of *Eretz Yisrael* as home, *Moledet*. No matter where they lived, no matter what the circumstances, Jews throughout time have been infused with a yearning for this special place and an aspiration to return some day to *Eretz Yisrael*.

The reality of the Land of Israel became increasingly remote after the destruction of the Second Temple and the failure of the Bar Kochba revolt.[3] As the Rabbis created the texts of the Mishnah, Talmud, and Midrash, they deliberately wrote about *Eretz Yisrael* in terms that conveyed its uniqueness and designation as a special land, chosen by God and where God's presence was most immanent.[4] Often, the Rabbis went to great lengths in talking about the Land of Israel, embellishing its holiness, identifying it as the center of the world, warning about the evils that would befall any Jew deserting it, and creating all manner of special rules about ritual and daily life that applied only within Israel. A few examples underscore this point.

- "He stood and measured the earth" (Hab. 3:6). The Holy One, blessed be He, measured all the nations and found the only one worthy of receiving the Torah was the generations of the wilderness.... He measured all the cities and found the only one worthy of housing the Temple was Jerusalem. He measured all the countries and found the only one worthy of being given to Israel was *Eretz Yisrael*.[5]

- When a man plasters his house, he should leave a small space unfinished in remembrance of Jerusalem. When a woman adorns herself with jewels, she should leave something off in remembrance of Jerusalem, as it is said: "If I forget you, O Jerusalem, let my right hand forget its cunning" (Ps. 137:5).[6]

- "The Lord loves the gates of Zion" (Ps. 87:2). In every city the king has a palace. Which one does he love the most? The palace which is in his own city. Said the Holy One: I love synagogues and houses of study. But what do I love even more than they? The gates of Zion, for that is My own palace.[7]

Alongside the legends and the laws that kept *Eretz Yisrael* and Jerusalem alive in the hearts of Jews throughout the world until the beginnings of Zionism and the resettlement of Israel, Jews lived as subjects in this land ruled by many different powers over time. Romans, Arabs, Crusaders, the Mamluk Empire, and the Ottoman Empire occupied this land, while a Jewish population waxed and waned depending on circumstances.[8] History records that there were as many as three hundred thousand Jews living under Muslim rule, most of whom were killed during the Crusades. Thus, while most Jews lived outside of *Eretz Yisrael* and had only an image projected through tradition, there was a continuous Jewish population in the land that came to be called Palestine, albeit a small one at various points in history.

Zionism and the Modern State of Israel

Zionism is a response to two developments that affected Jewish life in the nineteenth century. The first came in the wake of the Enlightenment and the Emancipation, which gave Jews citizenship in much of Western Europe. Jews responded to this newfound freedom and culture in a variety of ways, from self-imposed isolation to assimilation and conversion to the development of new forms of Judaism, such as Reform Judaism. It became clear, however, that even assimilation of Jews into the larger cultures in which they lived did not mitigate anti-Jewish sentiments.

The second development was the emergence of Italian and German national liberation movements. These movements provided a model of nationalism as an ideology and political force, as well as an impetus for the creation of Zionism, a national liberation movement for the Jewish people. Andre Oboler, spokesperson for the "Zionism on the Web Team," defines Zionism as follows:

> Zionism is the national revival movement of the Jews. It holds that Jews are a people and therefore have the right to self-determination in their own national home. It aims to secure and support a legally recognized national home for the Jews in their historical home-land, and to initiate and stimulate a revival of Jewish national life, culture, and language.[9]

Zionism assumed many different shapes. For some, it was the path to actualizing the religious yearnings and aspirations to return to *Eretz Yisrael*, leading to a formulation of religious Zionism. For others, Zionism was the political path to dealing with the antisemitism that plagued Europe even after Emancipation.

Theodore Herzl, the father of political Zionism, saw the establishment of a Jewish homeland as the solution.[10] Others merged their strong beliefs in socialism with national aspirations, advocating for Jews to return to the land in order to cultivate it with their own hands and labor. It is important to note that Zionism was never one monolithic ideological movement, but included variations from religious to socialist ideologies.[11]

The pioneers who came to Palestine to establish a homeland included waves of settlers, starting as early as 1878. They created early towns such as Rosh Pina and Rehovot on land purchased from Arab owners with the aid of Jewish philanthropy. In 1904 a new wave came, primarily from Eastern Europe. As socialist Zionists, they founded the first collective settlements, kibbutzim, which would prove critical in the establishment of an agricultural economy and socialist ideology for the emerging Jewish community. During the period of the British Mandate (1920–1946), in which the League of Nations entrusted the United Kingdom after World War I with some of the territories of the Ottoman Empire, including what is now Israel, Jordan, the West Bank, and Gaza, three more waves of settlers came. Then in 1939 the policy known as the British White Paper restricted Jewish immigration. The last wave included approximately 174,000 German Jews fleeing Nazism. Tragically, the British prevented many other Jews seeking refuge from genocide from entering Palestine.

Throughout the period of Jewish settlement there were tensions with Arab neighbors, but these tensions became particularly intense during the period of the British Mandate. They set the stage for the struggles that continue to the present day. On November 27, 1947, the United Nations voted to partition Palestine into Jewish and Arab states, but partition proved unacceptable to the Arabs. When the declaration of the establishment of the State of Israel was issued on May 15, 1948, the surrounding Arab countries invaded the newly born state.[12] This first war, called the War for Independence, became the first of four major wars that Israel fought when attacked by her Arab neighbors. The 1967 war, commonly known as the Six-Day War, is particularly important because Israel prevailed against the Jordanian troops and gained access to the Old City of Jerusalem, significant portions of the west bank of the Jordan River, the Gaza Strip, and the Sinai Peninsula. Israeli troops also occupied portions of the Golan Heights, which was Syrian territory and used consistently to attack Israeli settlements in the Northern Galilee.

Since 1967, many of these territories have been the basis of dispute with the Palestinians, because East Jerusalem, the West Bank, and Gaza have been under Israeli military control. The Sinai Peninsula was returned to Egypt as part of the Peace Treaty signed in 1979. In the summer of 2005, Israel withdrew from the Gaza Strip, turning control over to the Palestinian Authority.

These facts are important in understanding the complexity of the current situation in which Israel finds itself in regard to the Palestinians, the surrounding Arab countries, and those in the world who are quick to label Israel as an aggressive, "colonizing" power. Surrounded by large, well-equipped Arab armies who always were poised to attack, the early decades of Israel's history laid the groundwork for its overriding concern with security. The continuing struggle with the Palestinians, particularly the two protracted periods of terrorism (intifada, Arabic for "shaking off," or uprising)—one starting in 1987 and the second in 2000—have only increased the sense of vulnerability with which Israelis live every day.

Although relations with Arab countries in the region and with the Palestinians have consistently been a source of friction, it is important to remember that a significant percent of

Israeli citizens are non-Jews. According to the Central Bureau for Statistics of the State of Israel, the nation includes 1,072,500 Muslims, 115,700 Arab Christians, and 110,800 Druze.[13] As citizens, they have representation in the Israeli Parliament (*Knesset*) and other rights but, except for Druze citizens, cannot serve in the Israeli army. In a later section of this chapter, I will explore the political and social results of these realities. In spite of the many threats to its security, Israel has in its fifty-eight-year history achieved considerable success in nation-building. Like all First-World countries, Israel has social and economic problems with which it must deal, but its accomplishments in such a short amount of time are remarkable.

This short summary cannot do justice to the story of the creation of the State of Israel and the realization of Jews' two thousand years of longing to return to Jerusalem. Particularly in light of centuries of persecution, culminating in the Holocaust, and an enduring sense of being regarded as strangers wherever they lived, Jews could only rejoice when Israel was established. Jews throughout the world developed a new sense of Jewish pride. They celebrated Israel's victories and achievements and suffered through its struggles, identifying with the dangers Israel faced on a regular basis. They could move from the aspiration at the culmination of the Passover Seder—"Next Year in Jerusalem"—to boarding an El Al flight and coming to Jerusalem whenever they chose.

The story of the State of Israel comprises many tales. It is a tale of tragedy, because many Jews were denied access to Palestine when they might have been rescued from the ravages of the Holocaust. It is a tale of triumph, given the achievements of the early Zionist settlers who drained the swamps, battled disease, and learned how to water the desert with no preparation for the hardships they would endure or the new skills they would develop. It is a tale of fortitude, the challenge of a small nation not only to survive but also to prevail against an array

of enemies. Many works can fill in the details of this complicated story that I have briefly recounted.[14]

ISRAEL IN THE CHRISTIAN TRADITION: MARY

The Western face characteristic of Christianity in the modern
era, and its long association with colonialism so apparent in
this postmodern era, obscure an important reality: Christianity
originated in the Middle East, specifically in Jerusalem of
Roman-ruled Judea. It flourished throughout the region until
the Muslim conquest in the seventh century, regained power
for about ninety years through violent means during the
Crusades in the eleventh and twelfth centuries, and has
remained an important presence there as a minority tradition.
Today, however, the Christian presence throughout the Middle
East is much reduced. The factors involved in Christianity's
diminished presence are complex and vary from country to
country. Yet in focusing on Christians in relation to the Land
of Israel, it is important to situate them in the complex reality
of the cultural and political cauldron of the Middle East, past
and present.

The most obvious connection is to the land of Jesus of
Nazareth, a Galilean Jew who was crucified in Jerusalem in
April of the year 30 C.E., and whose followers, believing that
God raised Jesus from the dead, went out from Jerusalem into
the Mediterranean world and beyond, preaching the Gospel.
Yet when early Christians elected to retain the scriptures of the
Jews as theirs as well—the "Old" Testament—they shared with
Jews the memory of precious sites of biblical geography.
Eventually, the holy places Christians venerated became part of
a sacred landscape, what they came to call the Holy Land. It
took five centuries for this term to become critical to the
Christian imagination as perspectives evolved.[15]

Diverse views arose about Jerusalem. Above all in
Christian memory, Jerusalem was irrevocably linked to Jesus.

Although he was from the Galilee and much of his ministry took place in that region, the centripetal role his disciples gave to his passion, death, and resurrection—events that took place in Jerusalem—meant that the city figured prominently for them. Then, too, it was in an "upper room" in Jerusalem that the church began (Acts 1:12–14), and in Jerusalem that the first martyr, Stephen, was killed (Acts 7:54–60).

Jerusalem evoked eschatological tones, evident first in the Letter to the Hebrews. It became "heavenly Jerusalem" (12:22), and the author of Hebrews exhorted disciples to maintain their faith even in crisis: "For here we have no lasting city, but we are looking for the city that is to come" (13:14). For second-century Christian teachers Irenaeus (ca. 130–200) and Justin Martyr (ca. 100–165), the heavenly Jerusalem had a terrestrial correspondence: Jesus would return at the end of time to a rebuilt Jerusalem. In contrast, Origen of Alexandria (ca. 185–254) taught that the earthly Jerusalem symbolized heavenly bliss. Unlike the Jews, who longed for the restoration of the city, Origen believed that followers of Christ had no reason to desire that Jerusalem rise from the ashes of its destruction.

Inevitably, Christian perspective on Jerusalem and the land became part and parcel of its argument with Judaism that the Way of Jesus transcended and surpassed the Way of Torah.[16] This is evident particularly in Origen's conviction that because Christianity had eclipsed Judaism, Jewish claims to the physical land must give way to Christians' spiritualized interpretation. Scholars speculate that Origen may even have debated his views with Rabbi Yohanan ben Nappaha.[17] Moreover, the landscape seemed to corroborate Origen's theology. When Christian pilgrims began to visit Palestine in the fourth century, they viewed the ruins of a city and its magnificent Temple destroyed by Titus's army in 70 C.E. Emperor Hadrian renamed Jerusalem *Aelia Capitolina* after the Bar Kochba revolt in 135, and banned Jews from the city and all of Judea. Many

Christians regarded these events as confirmation of the rise of their faith and the demise of Judaism.

The rivalry with Judaism may be seen in the way early Christianity added a new layer to the cosmic symbolism of Jerusalem as the *axis mundi*, the navel of the earth. Texts in Ezekiel (5:5 and 38:12) seem to have first given rise to this, and it was embellished in later writings, such as the passage in Jubilees 8:19: "Mount Zion was in the midst of the navel of the earth," and in rabbinic literature.[18] Christian teachers added a new dimension. For example, Cyril, bishop of Jerusalem (349–384), preached in his "Catechetical Lectures" (13:28) about how Christ stretched out his hands on the cross to embrace "the ends of the world, for this Golgotha [the hill on which Jesus was crucified] is the very center of the earth." Sophronius, patriarch of Jerusalem when Muslims conquered that city in the seventh century, wrote in one of his poems:

> Let me walk your pavements
> And go inside the Anastasis[19]
> Where the King of all rose again
> Trampling down the power of death
> And as I venerate that worthy Tomb,
>
> Prostrate I will kiss the navel point of the earth,
>   that divine Rock
> In which was fixed the wood
> Which undid the curse of the tree
> How great your glory, noble Rock, in which was fixed
> The Cross, the Redemption of mankind.[20]

But more than rivalry with Judaism was at play in Christian attachment to the land. It was a living link to Jesus and his earliest followers: "If there were no places that could be seen and touched, the claim that God had entered human history could become a chimera."[21] The Judean desert attracted monks; eventually they established more than sixty monasteries, with about three thousand members. In the fourth and fifth centuries, pilgrims came in increasing numbers, showing great devotion to the holy places throughout the land and worshiping in various churches, including the great basilica built by Constantine. The piety of the pilgrims was tactile; place took on a sacramental dimension. Stational liturgies were celebrated at the various sites associated with the life and death of Jesus: at the Mount of Olives, at Golgotha, and at the Anastasis (tomb). Christians moved from site to site in public procession, singing hymns, praying, and chanting psalms. Their new public posture, as Robert Wilken observes, had serious ramifications:

> Space is never ideologically neutral. Jerusalem was becoming a Christian city, the city of the Christian God, and perforce a city of uncommon symbolic power for the Christian empire. As Jerusalem became a holy city it acquired a political as well as a religious character for Christians. If a hostile army should one day invade the city it would not only disrupt the public worship of God, but also threaten the stability of the Byzantine Empire.[22]

Indeed, a hostile army did invade in the middle of the seventh century. Muslim conquest ended Christian rule in Jerusalem in 638, although Christians continued to have a presence in the land. Christians lamented their loss in ways strikingly similar to Jewish lamentations over the destruction of the Temple in the sixth century B.C.E. and again in 70 C.E.

Tragically, after living in relative peace with Jews and Muslims, although not without tension, for some two centuries under Islamic rule, Christians transposed their laments into violence.[23] Pope Urban II, responding to the request of the emperor of Byzantium, Alexius I Comnenus, for military help against the Seljuk Turks in 1095, called for a "holy war" to liberate Christians in Asia Minor and the tomb of Christ in Jerusalem from Islam.[24] Thus, waves of crusading armies left Europe for the Middle East, slaughtering many Jews in the Rhineland en route. In conquering Jerusalem in 1099, "Muslims and Jews were cleared out of the Holy City like vermin."[25] Perhaps as many as thirty thousand were slaughtered, including Christians from the Eastern Orthodox tradition.

Crusades, major and minor, went on for more than four centuries against various perceived enemies, primarily against various Muslim groups (e.g., Seljuk Turks, Fatimids, Mamluks, Ottomans) but also against pagans and heretics. Jews, while not the principal antagonists, nevertheless were often touched by the violence. The Crusades ranged over a vast territory— from western Russia to the Nile Delta and from Portugal to Arabia—but it was Jerusalem and the Holy Land that dominated the imagination of the Crusaders.

The Crusades profoundly damaged Christian relationships with Muslims and Jews, as well as with Eastern Christians. This initial contact with the Christian West bequeathed to the Islamic world a longstanding legacy of mistrust of the West: "The religious imagination of millions of contemporary Muslims is shaped in part by the vividly preserved cultural memory of these brutal encounters with the so-called followers of the 'Prince of Peace.'"[26] The violence they suffered from the Crusaders also increased their devotion to Jerusalem (*al-Quds*, "the holy"), resulting in a more intensely Islamic city than had been the case before the attack of 1099.[27] Not only was the attack on the Jews of the Rhineland in 1096 the first full-blown pogrom in Europe, but it also "augured heightened tensions ahead."[28] Crusaders, after all, were those who "took the cross" (*crucesignati*), and under the banner of the cross, unspeakable deeds were justified. As a consequence, the cross, the preeminent symbol of Christianity, took on an ominous meaning, particularly for Jews.

Since Saladin's capture of Jerusalem in 1187, Christians have never been a powerful force in the Holy Land, though until quite recently, the Christian population has been significant. It is important, however, to recognize that Christianity in the Middle East encompasses a tremendous diversity of belief and practice. Unlike Christianity in the West, the Eastern Orthodox and Oriental Orthodox churches play leading roles, and each of those traditions is a complex mix of history, theology, cultures, and ethnicity.

Were we to map Christianity in the region today, it would look something like this:

- The Assyrian Church of the East

- The six Oriental Orthodox churches (Christian Coptic Church of Egypt, Eritrean Orthodox Church, Ethiopian Orthodox Church, Indian Orthodox Church, Syrian Orthodox Church of Antioch, and Armenian Orthodox Church), each independent but in communion with the others

- The Eastern Orthodox Church, a communion of national and regional churches who recognize the Patriarch of Constantinople (Istanbul) as the point of unity

- The Eastern Catholic churches, all in communion with the Roman Catholic Church; some of these churches are from the Oriental Orthodox churches and others are from the Orthodox Church

- The Latin or Roman Catholic Church

- The Evangelical (Protestant) and Anglican churches[29]

Although ecumenism is alive and well in many of these churches, the scars of centuries of mistrust and hostility have left their mark. The Church of the Holy Sepulchre, the successor to Constantine's Anastasis, bears this disfigurement in a dramatic way. As Jerome Murphy-O'Connor writes of the basilica in his archaeological guidebook:

> One expects the central shrine of Christendom to stand out in majestic isolation, but anonymous buildings cling to it like barnacles. One looks for numinous light, but it is dark and cramped. One hopes for peace, but the ear is assailed by a cacophony of warring chants. One desires holiness, only to encounter a jealous possessiveness: the six groups of occupants—Latin Catholics, Greek Orthodox, Armenians, Syrians, Copts, Ethiopians—watch one another suspiciously for any infringement of rights. The frailty of man [humankind] is nowhere more apparent than here; it epitomizes the human condition. The empty who come to be filled will leave desolate; those who permit the church to question them may begin to understand why hundreds of thousands thought it worthwhile to risk death or slavery in order to pray here.[30]

The Christian presence in the Holy Land has often been far from edifying; nevertheless, it is a living link to its origins:

> For Christians, the Holy Land is not simply an illustrious chapter in the Christian past. As Jerome wrote to his friend Paula in Rome urging her to come and live in the Holy Land, "The whole mystery of our faith is *native* to this country and city." Nothing else in Christian experience can make this claim; nothing has such fixity. No matter how many centuries have passed, no matter

> where the Christian religion has set down roots,
> Christians are wedded to the land that gave birth to
> Christ and the Christian religion.[31]

Today, however, this marriage to the land seems to be breaking up, as there has been a precipitous decline in the Christian population. In the early 1900s, the Christian population was estimated to be somewhere between 13 and 20 percent of the total population. In 2000, the estimate is that Christians constitute less than 2 percent of the population. In Jerusalem in 1944, for example, Christians numbered about thirty thousand during the British Mandate, a number that was drastically reduced from 1948–1967 when Jordan ruled part of the city; after the Six-Day War in 1967, when Israel captured East Jerusalem, there were about twelve thousand Christians. In 2000, there were no more than eight thousand Palestinian Christians left in Jerusalem. Some believe that the indigenous Christian community could disappear within two generations.

As journalist Charles Sennott writes in his riveting book, *The Body and the Blood,* the reasons for this decline are "layered and complex," but primarily due to greater opportunities for emigration from a land torn by strife. Palestinian Christians in general are better educated, in large part because of missionary schools, and are somewhat more affluent and better connected to Western churches than are Muslim Palestinians. Twice as many Christians from Ramallah live in Dearborn, Michigan, than in Ramallah. Three times as many Christians from Bethlehem live in the Palestinian Diaspora than live in Bethlehem.[32]

Among the implications of the diminished Christian presence is that Israeli Jews may know more about Christianity of the past—the Christianity of the Crusades and of pogroms and of complicity with the Nazis—than of Christianity in the present. As in virtually every matter between Jews and Christians, history is always on the table. In this case, however, history tends to overwhelm, complicating possibilities of reconciliation.

Sometimes a dramatic event suggests that the future can be different, as in the visit of Pope John Paul II to Israel on March 23–26, 2000. No longer the vigorous, athletic person of his earlier years, the frail pontiff met with Israeli political figures, with Jewish and Muslim religious leaders, and with the Armenian and Greek Orthodox patriarchs. He met with the then-president of the Palestinian Authority, Yasir Arafat, and toured a refugee camp. While he visited Christian holy sites throughout the country, he also prayed at the Western Wall, laid a wreath at *Yad Vashem* (the memorial to the victims of the Shoah), and met with the chief rabbis. He returned to Rome on the Israeli airline, El Al.

OUR INTERRELIGIOUS TRIO IN ISRAEL: MARY AND SARA

Our 1997 journey on El Al certainly pales in significance to the Pope's. We hold no offices of authority within our respective traditions and thus did not come as representatives on an official mission. We came as pilgrims. Yet, like Pope John Paul II, we wanted to meet persons and see sites beyond the borders of our own religious communities in Israel. We also wanted to learn from each other—to see this complicated country through the eyes of the other.

After we met up with Dorothy Bass in Tel Aviv, we set out in our rental car for the Galilee, where we stayed at *Kibbutz Nof Ginosar* on Lake Kinneret (Sea of Galilee) and joined in the festive celebration of Shabbat. Mary had stayed in this kibbutz on several other occasions, and she had vivid memories of meeting in 1986 the two brothers, Moshe and Yuval Lufan, who had discovered a first-century boat stuck in the mud in nearby Migdal (Magdala) when drought had reduced the lake's water level drastically. The boat has now undergone extensive treatment and is displayed in a museum on the kibbutz grounds.

Why such attention to a boat typical of those that plied the waters of Lake Kinneret in the first century? Aside from its archaeological significance, for Dorothy and Mary it evoked New Testament passages about Jesus being associated with boats.[33] This opened a lively, day-long conversation among the three of us about the ministry of Jesus as we visited other sites associated with him in the Galilee, such as the Mount of the Beatitudes and Tabgha, linked with the multiplication of loaves and fishes.[34]

As Sara led us to Qasrin, one of the oldest Jewish settlements in the Galilee, we had occasion to discuss the centrality of Galilee to Jewish survival after Hadrian expelled Jews from Judea in 135 C.E. From the second century until about 1000, Galilee served as the center for the Jewish community in Israel. From it came a rich rabbinic literature reflecting the vibrancy of Judaism, as well as many other artifacts of Jewish life.[35]

The juxtaposition of history in this land with the vibrancy of the modern State of Israel is fascinating. Close to Qasrin are some of the outstanding wineries of Israel, producing and exporting fine wines in an ever-growing industry.

From the relative calm of Galilee, we made our way to Jerusalem with a number of stops along the way. Driving through the bustling port city of Haifa, we experienced Israel as a First-World industrial center. Visiting the nearby small town of Ein Hod, we wandered through artists' galleries and mused over lunch about the emergence of the new national culture to which Zionism had aspired. In order to reach Jerusalem we drove along the "freeway" that parallels the coast and cuts through Tel Aviv. From the freeway we could see the large commercial buildings that are the heart of Israel's financial center, another sign of the economic success achieved in the some fifty years since the state was established.

Leaving the coast we began the climb, both physical and spiritual, to the bustling city of Jerusalem, which has rightly been described not as "*a* holy city but as a *multitude* of holy cities ... built over the same spot, operating at the same moment, and contending for hegemony."[36] In Jerusalem the sublime and the superficial meet, such as the Fourth Station T-Shirt Shop along the Via Dolorosa. So, too, do ancient and modern overlap: a donkey carries boxes of color television sets through the streets near the Damascus Gate; religious figures, garbed in traditional robes, carry on conversations on cell phones at each ear.

Even at some nine years' distance, we remember our intense conversations at our wonderful apartment on the Jerusalem campus of Hebrew Union College overlooking the Kidron Valley and the walls of the Old City near the Jaffa Gate. We discussed the history reflected in sites such as the Burnt House, Ecce Homo, and the Citadel. We reviewed sites we had walked that day, laughing over less edifying moments—it is a bit scandalous to be roughly pushed out of line by pious pilgrims eager to see Jesus's tomb! We shared misgivings: why Sara is ambivalent about the Western Wall and Mary about the church of the Holy Sepulchre.

It was important to us to visit sites in Jerusalem that are not only part of its ancient past but also critical to the recent history of the State of Israel. So we made our way to the Jerusalem neighborhood of *Ramat Eshkol*, controlled by the Jordanian Arab Legion until 1967. Many of Sara's friends and colleagues have lived in this area since the early 1970s because it is close to Mount Scopus and Hebrew University. In the midst of this pleasant residential area is a hilly park where one can view Ammunition Hill, site of one of the most important and bloodiest battles of the Six-Day War. Ammunition Hill held some of the strongest fortifications in Jerusalem, and the Israelis regarded it as a threat to Mount Scopus and the western half of the city. Many lives were lost before the Israelis could wrest control from the Jordanian Legionnaires. Thirty years later, we could appreciate the ferocity of the battle for control of Jerusalem.

No visit to Israel would be complete without a visit to the cemetery at *Har Herzl*. There the heroes of Israel's many wars are buried. It is there that Yitzhak Rabin, who had sought peace and for his efforts was assassinated by another Jew in 1995, was laid to rest. Walking the rows and reading the tombstones of so many young soldiers are powerful reminders of the blood that has been shed to defend Israel from its enemies. In a country with mandatory military service for all men and women at the age of eighteen, and many years of reserve duty to follow, the social and cultural life of adult Israelis is very much shaped by the experience of serving in the Israel Defense Forces (IDF).

We talked at length about what it means for Israel to be a Jewish country, a conversation initiated in part by Dorothy's surprise when she ventured out early on Sunday morning to discover that it was an ordinary day of work. We probed the intricacies of the Israeli political system and the complexities of the Israeli-Palestinian conflict. We spoke about what *Yad Vashem* evoked in us, particularly the children's memorial that had been recently completed. And as the week drew to a close, we lingered over the Shabbat table in view of the lighted walls of the Old City, knowing we had been privileged to be in this land together when so many of our ancestors in faith had fought over it.

THE CURRENT SITUATION: MARY

Just as Jerusalem is not simply a single city but a multitude of cities "built over the same spot, operating at the same moment, and contending for hegemony," so, too, is the question of Israel in relationship to the Palestinian people. Recently, at the conclusion of a brief lecture on Christian-Jewish relations I gave in Claremont, California, the first two questions from the audience focused on the political situation even though I had not mentioned it. In fact, the second questioner, who identified himself as a liberation theologian, seemed to me quite hostile to Israel. His perspective is not uncommon, especially in more liberal Christian circles, and is echoed in calls for denominations to divest themselves from companies in Israel.

The contentious matters involve the history of the creation of the State of Israel in 1948; international relations, including the various United Nations Resolutions (overwhelmingly condemnatory of Israel) and the peace treaties (e.g., Oslo Peace Accords of 1993 and 1995, the 1998 Wye Agreement); the political posture of the Israeli governments and of the Palestinian Authority; the political stance of the governments of surrounding Arab nations; the antagonism toward Jews, Judaism, and Zionism among many Muslims and particularly among Islamists; and the role of the United States and other Western nations.

The security barrier or wall or fence Israel is building to ward off terrorist attacks illustrates many of the complexities. For some, it is a security barrier. It has also been a factor in a significant reduction in terrorist attacks. For others, it is a wall that separates. The wall infringes on Palestinian life, bisecting neighborhoods and inflicting economic damage. Many of Israel's critics deplore the wall and condemn the government for continuing to build it. Muslim writer Irshad Manji says she hears it described as "Ariel Sharon's apartheid wall" and that this is a "phrase spoken—make that spewed—on almost every university campus I visit in North America and Europe." During a visit to the West Bank town of Abu Dis, Manji observed the hardships the wall imposed on the people. She notes the anti-Israel graffiti Western activists have inscribed: "Scotland hates the blood-sucking Zionists." But when she asks a Palestinian man about the suicide bombers, he refuses to answer. His silence evokes Manji's response:

Like all Muslims, I look forward to the day when neither the jeep [of Israeli soldiers] nor the wall is in Abu Dis. So will we tell the self-appointed martyrs of Islam that the people—not just Arabs, but Arabs and Jews—"are one"? That before the barrier, there was the bomber? And that the barrier can be dismantled, but the bomber's victims are gone forever.[37]

In light of all the complexities, it is tempting simply to admit my lack of expertise, and to take refuge in generalities. But since I am increasingly asked about Israel and the Palestinians, let me sketch the context in which I think about this vexing issue, even as I fear no one will find my viewpoint satisfactory. I will list various points, as if I were responding to a questioner in as succinct a manner as the issues will allow:

- We Christians have no moral high ground from which to speak. Many Christians tend either to speak uncritically of Israel (the Christian Zionism of many Evangelicals) or to speak in righteous judgment of Israel (some liberal Christians). Both stances are problematic. Too few of us know how firmly Augustine's dictum that the Jews were condemned to perpetual wandering has been embedded in our tradition. Too few of us know the complexity of the Middle East, past and present, including the bloody hands of "our" Crusaders. Too few of us understand Christian complicity in antisemitism through centuries of disparagement of Judaism and vilification of Jews by the church. Too few of us grapple with how Christian missionary attempts to convert Jews further reduce a people who lost six million in the Nazi genocide.

• One would at times think that the Arab-Israeli conflict were the only clash between two peoples, given the disproportionate attention it garners.

• Moral purity is not possible on the Arab-Israeli conflict, and binary categories, such as oppressor/oppressed, are distinctly unhelpful. False comparisons (Israel as an "apartheid state") oversimplify the situation and are also not helpful.

• The land, and particularly Jerusalem, is at the core of Jewish liturgy, poetry, and mythos. Although large numbers of Ashkenazi (European) Jews emigrated after the creation of the State of Israel in 1948, Judaism is profoundly rooted in the Middle East, and many Sephardic Jews have emigrated from (or been expelled from) Arab lands. To speak of Israel as "colonizing" Palestine falsifies history. Jews lived continuously in the land for thousands of years, almost always under foreign rule. And when they came in greater numbers after World War II, they did not arrive as colonists, eager to exploit the resources, but instead as builders of a nation.

• I believe that the State of Israel has a right to exist. I also believe in a "two-state solution": Both Israel and the Palestinian people have a right to live within secure and just borders.

• Both Israelis and Palestinians have just causes, often championed in unjust ways. Both peoples have endured tremendous suffering and have inflicted suffering on the other.

• The Palestinian people have been ill-served by their leaders, especially by the corruption of Yasir Arafat and his Fatah Movement.[38] Suicide bombings and other acts of Palestinian terrorism have elicited harsh reprisals from the Israelis, and the cycle of violence, particularly that unleashed by the two uprisings (intifada), seems ever more deadly. The tough measures Israelis employ for their security are a constant source of humiliation and economic hardship for Palestinians and have a dehumanizing effect on those who must enact them.[39]

• The election on January 29, 2006, which resulted in the Hamas Movement attaining 56 percent of the seats in the Palestinian Parliament, complicates the already thorny situation. Classified by the European Union and the United States as a terrorist organization, Hamas is dedicated to Israel's destruction. Article 7 of its Covenant reads: "The Day of Judgment will not come about until Moslems fight Jews and kill them." Hamas also blames Jews for virtually all the violence in the world: "There is no war going on anywhere without them [the Jews] having their finger in it" (article 22).

• Israel is a tiny land (8,463 square miles, about one-sixth the size of the state of Michigan) in a hostile region in which Holocaust denial and hatred of Jews, Zionism, and Israel have become a rhetorical trope. When Iran's president, Mahmoud Ahmadinejad, called for "Israel to be wiped off the face of the map" at a "World Without Zionism" seminar on October 26, 2005, he was echoing sentiments firmly embedded in that country's leadership since the revolution led by Ayatollah Khomeini in 1979, and with many parallels in other Muslim nations.

• The Arab-Israeli conflict is primarily a political, not a religious, conflict. Religious extremists, however, compound the problems, especially those religious leaders who call for or support violence in the name of religion.

• The Shoah looms large, perhaps more so for Ashkenazi Jews than for Sephardic Jews. In chapter 6, Sara cites Irving Greenberg, who summarizes this well: "The reborn State of Israel is the fundamental act of life and meaning after Auschwitz. To fail to grasp that inextricable connection and response is to fail to comprehend the theological significance of Israel."[40]

• Greenberg has written eloquently about the "ethic of power" critical to Jewish survival. But, as John Pawlikowski challenges, such an ethic requires the balance of an "ethic of solidarity," in which the Shoah sensitizes Jews to the plight of Palestinians, lest they create Palestinian "expendables."[41]

• The region desperately needs wise, skillful leaders, but the Middle East has not been kind to leaders who took dramatic strides for peace, such as Anwar Sadat and Yitzhak Rabin, both of whom were assassinated.

• Palestinian Christians, generally better educated and with more resources, can serve as a bridge between Muslims and Jews. The Sabeel Ecumenical Liberation Theology Center seeks to bring Christian liberation thought to the Arab-Israeli conflict. Yet liberation theologies, for all their sensitivity to suffering peoples, tend to work in the binaries of oppressor and oppressed. For example, when some of the Sabeel leaders use language about the cross of Jesus to reflect on Palestinian suffering, their rhetoric alludes to Jewish responsibility for the death of Jesus—an accusation that Christian churches have rejected for the past half century. Consider the 2001 Easter message of Reverend

Naim Ateek, Sabeel's president who is an Arab-Israeli citizen and an Anglican priest:

> Jesus is on the cross again with thousands of crucified Palestinians around him. It only takes people of insight to see the hundreds of thousands of crosses throughout the land, Palestinian men, women, and children being crucified. Palestine has become one huge Golgotha. The Israeli government crucifixion system is operating daily. Palestine has become the place of the skull.[42]

The hyperbole of the "Israeli crucifixion system" does nothing to build bridges, and it verges on once again characterizing Jews as "Christ-killers."

• Many persons "on the ground" have been laboring for peace and reconciliation for many years, and their efforts get far too little publicity. Deep and abiding relationships between Jews and Palestinians of all ages have been forged, thanks to institutions such as Seeds for Peace, the Interreligious Coordinating Council in Israel, Peace Now, and Coalition of Women for Peace. It is imperative that we invest in such organizations.

In short, we have good reason to pray, as the psalmist taught us, "Pray for the peace of Jerusalem: 'May they prosper who love you. Peace be within your walls, and security within your towers'" (Ps. 122:6–7). For the sake of my relatives and friends I will say, "Peace be within you."

THE CURRENT SITUATION: SARA

It is Passover 2006. As I ponder what I can say about the current situation in Israel, I am surrounded by paradoxes. Perhaps the most promising approach from a Jewish perspective is a personal one. My granddaughter Maya has just returned from a two-week trip to Israel with her eighth-grade peers from her Jewish day school. It was exciting and inspiring. She made new friends with families from Haifa's Reali School, which is the partner school to her own, spent Shabbat with family friends in Jerusalem, and returned home committed to spending a year in Israel after high school, as her parents and uncles did in their time. Maya is only fourteen years old, but this was her third trip to Israel.

I traveled to Israel in January 2006, my first long trip after being confined to a cast and a wheelchair from an accident in August 2005. I have gone to Israel each year to conduct a mid-year colloquium for first-year students at Hebrew Union College. My friends and colleagues pleaded with me not to travel this past January in light of my recent recovery. They could not persuade me, so intent was I on returning to Israel once more, despite my anxiety about navigating Hebrew Union College's campus and the streets of Jerusalem. For me, landing at Ben Gurion Airport is always a kind of homecoming.

During the Passover holiday I was reading Hirsh Goodman's column in *The Jerusalem Report*. Goodman, a regular columnist whom I always find insightful, reflected on the decline in invitations to him and other "Israel experts" to speak at dinners and conventions sponsored by Jewish communities around the world. Goodman heard from a friend in a similar situation who learned from his agent: "Those responsible for providing content at Jewish events were now going for comedians; that they now found Israel depressing and boring and that threats from a nuclear Iran and the ascendancy of Hamas were hardly entertaining." Goodman concludes, "This is the time to change the atmosphere. One cannot live on bad news forever. The mind and soul need a break and, despite the clouds, things are looking up."[43]

The very next day after reading this column filled with wit and irony, I opened the newspaper to the report of a suicide bombing in Tel Aviv, which killed nine innocent people buying lunch at a small restaurant in a working-class neighborhood. The Islamic Jihad claimed responsibility, but the Hamas-led Palestinian government defended the bombing. How does a Jew who cares deeply about Israel maintain a balance on this roller-coaster ride that best describes the reality of Israel in its current situation?

The roots of the current struggles between Israel and the Palestinians predate the establishment of the State of Israel. The history of the conflict is well documented.[44] At the heart of the ongoing conflict are two opposing views. From an Israeli perspective, Israel is the historic homeland of the Jewish people. The Zionists who shaped its political, social, and cultural life believed strongly that it should be a modern state founded on justice, independence, and democracy. There has always been a struggle over the role of religion in the state.

On the other hand,

> the dominant Arab view is that the Jewish community in Palestine was the colonial creation of a European colonial regime, Great Britain. In this view, the State of Israel continues to be a colonial presence in the Middle East.... It suggests that political leaders are not indigenous to the region but nevertheless control the state.[45]

There is little doubt that these two very different views are irreconcilable. When Hamas leaders continue to call for the destruction of the State of Israel, there appears little hope that there will be peace or reconciliation between Israel and the Palestinian people. When political extremists within Israel demand that Israel must control all the land described in biblical accounts of the "Promised Land" while ignoring the reality of Palestinians living in many of these areas, there is also cause for despair. There are few signs that peace will emerge from this conflict—and ample tragedy on both sides.

Although the most extreme pronouncements by both Israelis and Palestinians dominate the headlines, the reality is that among many Israelis, as evidenced by the victory of the Kadimah Party in the March 2006 elections, the prevailing sentiment is the desire for security and relief from continuing terrorist threats. Israelis are ready to give up land to achieve this goal. In the face of a Palestinian government that challenges the legitimacy of the State of Israel—a stance I believe many Palestinians would reject in exchange for economic and national security—there is little room for negotiation. The stance of disengagement, advocated by the Kadimah Party and its leader Ehud Olmert, is perhaps the only efficacious path that Israel can follow to define its defensible boundaries and move away from being an occupying military presence in the midst of the Palestinians. Although this is a far cry from peace, it may be the best we can hope for at this time.

In many ways, Mary's observations about the current situation, albeit written from a Christian perspective, parallel my own. For me and many other Jews, however, Israel is a powerful personal connection that shapes our lives as Jews. It is visceral. Israel has a very special place in my heart. It was my formative year in Israel as a student that shaped my self-understanding as a Jew. Israel has been an ongoing presence in the life of my children and grandchildren. The students whom I teach have all spent their first year of study at Hebrew Union College in Israel. Neither terrorism nor disability has prevented me from going to Israel regularly.

The tragedies of the Israeli-Arab and Israeli-Palestinian conflict are the cause of great pain, and I hope for the day when compromise will benefit all. Although there is a broad spectrum of political views among Jews, I believe we all share a conviction that Israel must survive and be secure. The Jewish future is unimaginable without Israel. I do not believe that

Jews need to defend the right of Israel to exist to any person or group. My hopes are focused on Israel being able to redirect its energies from military preoccupation to the prosperity and welfare of its citizens.

The Jewish tradition places much stock in hope. Our history demands it. *Eretz Yisrael* embodied our dreams of hope, even in the midst of great suffering. It is no surprise that the national anthem of the State of Israel is *"Hatikvah,"* "The Hope." During these times, hope is the only response we can have to the ongoing struggle of two peoples for this special place that has spawned many of the great religious ideas that have shaped humanity.

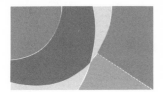

8

PARTICIPANTS SPEAK:
TESTIMONY TO THE POWER OF
INTERRELIGIOUS LEARNING

As we planned the various chapters in this book, it seemed fitting to conclude with voices from participants in our various projects. We had extensive material from the external, professional evaluation of the Catholic-Jewish Colloquium, some correspondence from participants from whom we heard on occasion, and notes compiled by an interviewer whom we hired to do follow-up with eight persons. We make no pretense of offering a rigorously structured evaluation. Rather, we offer a sampling of what participants have told us.

Many told us how important it is for persons to step outside their familiar worlds and to risk entering into the more threatening realm of interreligious dialogue. This requires "the ability and willingness to make yourself vulnerable, to be ready to realize that you don't have it all, but that's O.K." In a similar vein, another spoke about how he was struck by the importance of the virtue of humility, of recognizing the limits of religious traditions in engaging the transcendent or the Divine. Still another emphasized the significance for her of paying attention—"I mean paying real close attention"—to the other. One person expressed, "We need to see ourselves through the eyes of the other, and develop the discipline and patience to see the other through their own eyes. That happens when we are in dialogue with real people who embody the tradition." Her comments were echoed: "I met a group of Catholics who cared passionately about who they are and are self-critical. And Jews who were very open and had to own some of our own bigotry. And I think it made me a more religious person because I saw other possibilities than what I knew."

A Jewish academic reported, "I became more committed to and vocal about the need for Jewish educators to devote time and create opportunities to come to better understand other faith traditions. It is not only important, but critical." A similar sentiment, though expressed in the negative, came from a Catholic academic, who worried: "I am more and more convinced that the direction of religious education in our communities is somewhat myopic. Just as the times are calling us to be more cognizant of our relationship with the other," those religions that give "a certain false sense of security" by claiming to have the full truth "are what appeal to many people." Her judgment was echoed by another who remarked that "our own [Catholic] tradition has a tendency to flatten or make one-dimensional the richness and multidimensionality of the tradition. We tend to like simple, clean-cut answers."

We heard again and again, "It was in the interaction that the power was most evident. It was the strength of this project." Another said, "I think the incredible depth and commitment and sincerity of the other participants had a dramatic effect on me." One remarked simply: "It made me more confident in reaching out to the other, and open in them reaching out to me." A participant told us that much of the Colloquium was "challenging each other beyond our comfort zones. Over time, people were willing to do that—to open sides of their religious life and communities. It really became a community because there was openness to each other."

One of the more important outcomes for many was a new sense of the depth of the scriptures. "I remember reading a psalm about Jerusalem with Jewish educators and the power of seeing this text [through the eyes] of those for whom the text first had meaning." She added, "I have learned from my Jewish colleagues a reverence for the text. There is something about the care with texts that is characteristic of Jewish ways that I found enriching and powerful. It has helped me read any text with particular care to the shape of the words and forms of language." Another woman told us that one of the "great gifts" of the project was reading biblical texts in a fuller context. She added that when she reads from the psalms or prophets now she finds a "different way" of understanding them. Several remarked on the need for Christians to do more intensive work on the "Old" Testament and, if at all possible, to study it with Jews. And just as many Christians came to appreciate Jewish knowledge of texts, Jews came to appreciate the ease with which Christians spoke of their faith.

Those with whom we communicated have told us how much interreligious learning enhanced their sense of their *own* tradition. One said, "I think that one of the things the seminar did was to help me understand my own tradition in a much more nuanced way." A Catholic told us, "While I learned a lot about Judaism and was nourished by the Jews I met, it was the understanding of my own Christianity … that impacted me most dynamically." Her testimony was echoed by a Jew: "It made me appreciate my own tradition even more. It made me have to dig for answers I hadn't had to look at before, to see what's missing in our tradition that may be worth pursuing." As another participant said, "I was being stretched and opened up to my own religious life and given a window into others. I think it matured me as a human being. In terms of my development, this was one of the most powerful experiences I have had, and it continues to direct my interest." He continued that the experience "profoundly" affected his identity:

> I think it opened up for me parts of my own Jewish tradition that I would not have explored or even discovered if it were not for the opportunity to see that played out in a different context. Things like sacrifice, incarnation, embodiment, love, and salvation—things that I would often have associated with Christianity without exploring the ways Judaism has serious commitments to the same constructs in different ways.

For Christian participants in our projects, it was a challenge to confront the polemical aspect of the New Testament and to face the anti-Judaism that runs so strongly through their tradition. One person told us that when she understood this, "I became vigilant, almost militant, when I heard people talk disparagingly about Jews." In time, she reports, her militancy "softened," as she came to realize that building relationships and entering into dialogue makes change more possible. Another told us that "Christians have to unlearn a tendency to overlook our limitations when we are encountering the other because 'we have the truth.'" Likewise, we learned that for one woman the exposure to the shadow side of Christianity "coincided with [the sexual abuse] scandals in the church and rightward trends," both of which, she said, "have made it more difficult for me to claim my own tradition." She reports being "less hesitant to raise critical questions" about her tradition.

Some of the participants in our projects are professionally positioned to give extensive leadership in interreligious understanding, and they report leading various institutes or centers. Some are reaching out to other institutions. Others integrate their experience in the projects into their own teaching.

Another, who gave birth to two children in the immediate wake of the Colloquium, brought a group of Christian and Jewish mothers together monthly. At the initial session, each mother spoke about what she hoped to gain. One woman said that her hope was, "If there was another Holocaust, that one of you would hide me." Our participant remarked: "To touch that raw vulnerability. You could hear the gasp from the other women in the room." A Jewish participant is now enrolled in a doctoral program in a Catholic university run by the Society of Jesus (the Jesuits). He says he never would have considered that prior to his participation, which not only increased his comfort level with non-Jews but also enabled him to come to know a Jesuit priest, who is on the faculty where he has matriculated.

One of our participants dreams of creating "interreligious model communities where we are actually living together in a school or camp setting." He wants to take interreligious learning to another level "where it is happening in an organic, natural, frequent way."

Nothing could make the two of us happier than interreligious learning rising to new and more expansive levels.

NOTES

CHAPTER 1

Jews and Christians: A Complicated Relationship

1. Hans Küng, *Global Responsibility: In Search of a New World Ethic* (London: SCM Press, 1991), 105.

2. See Diana Eck, *A New Religious America: How a "Christian Country" Has Become the World's Most Religiously Diverse Nation* (San Francisco: HarperSanFrancisco, 2001).

3. Craig S. Smith, "Paris Journal: Poor and Muslim? Jewish? This Soup Is Not for You," *The New York Times* (February 28, 2006): 1.

4. Rabbi Jonathan Sacks, *To Heal a Fractured World: The Ethics of Responsibility* (New York: Schocken, 2005), 9. For an excellent study of the role religion plays in violence, see Mark Juergensmeyer, *Terror in the Mind of God: The Global Rise of Religious Violence* (Berkeley: University of California Press, 2001).

5. Jonathan Sacks, *The Dignity of Difference: How to Avoid the Clash of Civilizations* (London: Continuum, 2002), 43.

6. For this decree and its context, see Jacques Dupuis, S.J., *Toward a Christian Theology of Religious Pluralism* (Maryknoll, NY: Orbis Books, 1997), 84–109.

7. On Vatican II, see John M. Oesterreicher, "Declaration on the Relationship of the Church to Non-Christian Religions," in *Commentary on the Documents of Vatican II,* vol. 3, ed. Herbert Vorgrimler (New York: Herder and Herder, 1969), 1–137; Arthur Gilbert, *The Vatican Council and the Jews* (Cleveland: World Publishing, 1968); and Ormond Rush, *Still Interpreting Vatican II: Some Hermeneutical Principles* (New York: Paulist Press, 2004). For a superb analysis of the spectrum of views within Christianity, see Paul F. Knitter, *Introducing Theologies of Religions* (Maryknoll, NY: Orbis, 2002).

8. See www.phc.edu/about/default.asp. See also Hanna Rosin, "God and Country," *The New Yorker* (June 27, 2005): 44–49.

9. *Tosefta, Avodah Zarah*, 8:4; Babylonian Talmud, *Sanhedrin*, 56a, 60a.

10. *Sifra* on Leviticus 19:18.

11. The Mishnah, an authorized compilation of rabbinic law, was promulgated ca. 210 C.E. by Rabbi Judah Ha-Nasi. The Talmud, two versions of rabbinic law, including the Mishnah and additional commentaries and discussion, was compiled by Jerusalem scholars around the early fourth century C.E. and by Babylonian scholars around the fifth century C.E.

12. Elliot N. Dorff, "A Jewish Theology of Jewish Relations to Other Peoples," in *People of God, Peoples of God: A Jewish-Christian Conversation in Asia,* ed. Hans Ucko (Geneva, Switzerland: World Council of Churches, 1996), 56.

13. David Ellenson, "A Jewish Legal Authority Addresses Jewish-Christian Dialogue: Two Responsa of Rabbi Moshe Feinstein," *The American Jewish Archives Journal,* 52/1–2 (Cincinnati: Jacob Rader Marcus Center of the American Jewish Archives, 2000): 113–128; citation, 122.

14. Ellenson, "A Jewish Legal Authority," 117. For papers from a 2003 symposium on Soloveitchik at Boston College, see www.bc.edu/research/cjl/meta-elements/texts/center/conferences/soloveitchik/.

15. Irving Greenberg, "Pluralism and Partnership," *From the Martin Buber House* 26 (Heppenheim, Germany: Martin Buber House, 1999): 76.

16. Greenberg, "Pluralism and Partnership," 76.

17. Dorff, "A Jewish Theology," 61.

18. "Winning Hearts through Minds," *A Campaign for Equity: 2004 Annual Report* (New York: Teachers College, Columbia University, 2004): 26.

19. See Diana Eck, *Encountering God: A Spiritual Journey from Bozeman to Banaras* (Boston: Beacon Press, 1993), 194–198.

20. Jean Halperin, cited in Eck, *Encountering God*, 189.

21. Sacks, *The Dignity of Difference*, 201.

22. David Ellenson, "Interreligious Learning and the Formation of Religious Identity," *Religious Education* (1994). This article is available online at: www.bc.edu/research/cjl/meta-elements/sites/partners/erpp/CJC_Ellenson.htm.

23. See Mary C. Boys, "Anti-Judaism and Antisemitism: A Complicated Convergence," in *Rebuilding the Broken Bridges between Christians and Jews*, ed. Irvin Borowsky (Philadelphia: Crossroad, 2004), 47–62.

24. Most of our work together has been with Catholics, although we have done (and continue to do) events with a variety of Christian denominations. The more varied the denominational mix, the more complicated it is to educate.

CHAPTER 2

Sara's Story

1. Arnold J. Band, "Confluent Myths," in *Judaism and Education: Essays in Honor of Walter I. Ackerman*, ed. Haim Marantz (Israel: Ben-Gurion University Press of the Negev, 1998), 3.

2. John F. Stack, *International Conflict in an American City: Boston's Irish, Italians and Jews 1935–1944* (Westport, CT: Greenwood Press, 1979). See also Jenny Goldstein, "Transcending Boundaries: Boston's Catholics and Jews, 1929–1965" (Senior Honors Thesis, Brandeis University, 2001).

3. Goldstein, "Transcending Boundaries," 17.

4. These comments are based on interviews with my brother, Joel Schwartz, Ph.D., who recently retired from the faculty of the University of North Carolina at Chapel Hill. His field is political science, with specialization in Eastern European political structures of the twentieth century.

5. Goldstein, "Transcending Boundaries," 15.

6. Mary C. Boys, *Has God Only One Blessing? Judaism as a Source of Christian Self-Understanding* (New York: Paulist Press, 2000), 249.

7. This was the first of many occasions on which I would study this book that would shape my understanding of Zionism and Judaism. See Arthur Hertzberg, *The Zionist Idea* (New York: Atheneum, 1959).

8. This insight is particularly important in that I was not ready to engage seriously with another faith until I felt secure in my own. The awareness of the necessity of a grounded particularism for any kind of interreligious learning and commitment to religious pluralism was borne out by our experience with the Catholic-Jewish Colloquium. See Mary C. Boys and Sara S. Lee, "The Catholic-Jewish Colloquium: An Experiment in Interreligious Learning," *Religious Education* 91/4 (Fall 1996): 421–466.

9. For more information on the Institute for Youth Leaders from Abroad (*Machon L'Madrichei Chutz La'aretz*), see www.jafi.org.il/education/study/hadracha/machon.html.

10. For a description of this period of Israel's history, see Tom Segev, *1949: The First Israelis* (New York: The Free Press, 1986), 95–116, and Howard M. Sachar, *A History of Israel* (New York: Knopf, 1976), 395–428.

11. For more information on Hadassah, see www.hadassah.org.

12. The youth groups, camps, and Israel programs of Young Judaea are described on their website at www.youngjudaea.org. Although new programs have been added over the years, the core programs remain much the same as when my children participated in the 1970s and 1980s.

13. For a more extensive discussion about the differing perspectives on Israel and the ensuing tensions, see Marc Saperstein, *Moments of Crisis in Jewish-Christian Relations* (Philadelphia: Trinity Press International, 1989), 55–59, and Christopher M. Leighton, Donald G. Dawe, and Avi Weinstein, "What Is the Meaning of

'Israel' for Jews and Christians?" in *Irreconcilable Differences?* ed. David M. Sandmel, Rosann M. Catalano, and Christopher M. Leighton (Boulder: Westview Press, 2001), 91–111.

14. For this paper, I read a number of books and articles about Christianity, the New Testament, and Paul. Of particular importance were W. D. Davies, *Paul and Rabbinic Judaism* (New York: Harper and Row, 1967); Samuel Sandmel, *A Jewish Understanding of the New Testament* (New York: University Publishers, 1956); and E. P. Sanders, "Patterns of Religion in Paul and Rabbinic Judaism: A Holistic Approach," *Harvard Theological Review* 66 (1973): 455–478.

15. Alexander Roberts and James Donaldson, eds., *Anti-Nicene Fathers,* vol. 1 (Peabody, MA: Hendrickson Publishers, 2004), 137–149.

16. See the NCCJ website at www.nccj.org.

17. Ramona Convent Secondary School is conducted by the Sisters of the Holy Names, the religious order to which Mary belongs.

18. Sara S. Lee, "Repairing the World from the Perspective of Jewish Tradition," *Religious Education* 85/3 (Summer 1990): 402–410, and Sara S. Lee, "An Educational Perspective on Interreligious Dialogue: Jewish View," *Religious Education* 86/2 (Spring 1991): 184–196.

CHAPTER 3

Mary's Story

1. This chapter builds from an earlier essay, "The Road Is Made by Walking," in *Faith Transformed: Christian Encounters with Jews and Judaism,* ed. John C. Merkle (Collegeville: Liturgical Press, 2003), 162–181. Used by permission.

2. *A Catechism of Christian Doctrine Prepared and Enjoined by Order of the Third Plenary Council of Baltimore,* No. 3 (New York: Benziger Brothers, 1921), 79 (Q & A 391). This is the "Baltimore Catechism," first published in 1885 and revised in 1941 (Q & A 391 remain unchanged in the 1941 revision).

3. See Mary C. Boys, *Educating in Faith: Maps and Visions* (San Francisco: HarperSanFrancisco, 1989), 94–95.

4. *A Catechism of Christian Doctrine,* 97 (A 487).

5. *Pacem in Terris*, #41. See www.papalencyclicals.net/John23/ j23pacem.htm.

6. Several years ago I was asked—by a Vatican official, no less—to give a paper on feminism in the church at a Catholic-Jewish conference in London. I gave it the title "Loving a Church That Squanders the Gifts of Its Women: A Lament."

7. *Nostra Aetate*, #2. See www.vatican.va/archive/ hist_councils/ii_vatican_council/documents/ vat-ii_decl_19651028_nostra-aetate_en.html.

8. In common parlance, this is "entering the convent." I regret, however, that we ever used such a term, as it obscures the reality that we have joined our lives to others in our desire for God and what God desires for all creation. It is not about entering a place, but a people.

9. During this period, one of the leaders of Vatican II, Belgian Leon Cardinal Suenens, published a book that influenced us significantly, *The Nun in the World: Religious and the Apostolate* (New York: Newman, 1963).

10. One of the sixteen documents promulgated by Vatican II, *Perfectae Caritatis*, dealt with the renewal of religious life.

11. In its earliest years, our congregation conducted schools for girls from families of limited means. Educating the "poor and disadvantaged" remains a central focus of our mission.

12. The states of Oregon and Washington have the highest percentage of persons who do not affiliate with a church. See Martin B. Bradley, et al., *Churches and Church Membership in the United States 1990* (Atlanta: Glenmary Research Center, 1992).

13. See Michael Brown, "From Stereotype to Scapegoat: Anti-Jewish Sentiment in French Canada from Confederation to World War I," and Pierre Anctil, "Interlude of Hostility: Judeo-Christian Relations in Quebec in the Interwar Period, 1919–39," in *Antisemitism in Canada: History and Interpretation*, ed. Alan T. Davies (Ottawa: Wilfrid Laurier University Press, 1992), 39–66 and 135–166, respectively. In general, Jews were regarded as outsiders and a threat to the status quo of the Anglo-Protestant and French-Catholic arrangement. Anctil summarizes:

No matter how the Jewish community defined its social aspirations, it was bound to be marginalized by virtue of its spiritual deviation, or at best held hostage by one of the two dominant confessions to which it was forced to submit for educational reasons. To many Christians, Jews appeared as a force bent on destroying a political status quo achieved with great difficulty, a fragile yet viable social consensus in a country where military conquest and the subjugation of one European colonial tradition by another had left deep cleavages…. Among French Canadians in particular, a constant feeling of vulnerability added extra weight to the fear that their national identity would be weakened, once its religious and institutional safeguards had been removed. Were not French Canadians first and foremost Catholics, and was not Catholicism the protector of the French language? Surely the Roman church, dominated by a conservative clerical elite, was of the utmost importance in the struggle for cultural survival (152).

14. See William Least Heat-Moon, *Blue Highways: A Journey into America* (New York: Little, Brown, 1999). Originally published in 1982.

15. Sandra M. Schneiders, *Finding the Treasure: Locating Catholic Religious Life in a New Ecclesial and Cultural Context,* vol. 1 (New York: Paulist Press, 2000), 138–144, 348.

16. Schneiders, *Finding the Treasure,* 330.

17. Celibacy seems to have been characteristic only of the Therapeutae, a first-century Jewish ascetic group near Alexandria, Egypt. Scholars debate whether the covenanters at Qumran were celibate and, if so, whether that was a permanent or temporary state. Cf. Lawrence Schiffman, *Reclaiming the Dead Sea Scrolls* (New York: Doubleday, 1994), 127–143, and Joseph Fitzmyer, *Responses to 101 Questions on the Dead Sea Scrolls* (New York: Paulist Press, 1992), 66.

18. For an analysis of this reticence, including its problematic character, see Steven M. Cohen and Arnold M. Eisen, *The Jew Within: Self, Family and Community in America* (Bloomington: Indiana University Press, 2000), esp. chapter 6, "God and the Synagogue," 155–180.

19. Abraham Joshua Heschel, *The Prophets* (New York: Harper & Row, 1962). German original, 1936. See John Merkle, ed.,

Abraham Joshua Heschel: Exploring His Life and Thought (New York: Macmillan, 1985).

20. Schneiders draws upon Heschel in her theology of religious life. Heschel viewed the prophet's fundamental experience as a "fellowship with the feelings of God, a sympathy with the divine pathos." Schneiders argues that the immediacy to God and marginality to the social order fundamental to religious life cultivate "participation in the divine pathos." "To feel the pathos of God," she continues, "is not a warm and comfortable religious experience; it is an experience of the howling wilderness driving one to protest" (*Finding the Treasure*, 139, 141).

21. See Mary C. Boys, "*Heilsgeschichte* as a Hermeneutical Principle in Religious Education" (Doctoral dissertation, Teachers College, Columbia University, 1978). This was later published in revised form as *Biblical Interpretation in Religious Education: A Study of the Kerygmatic Era* (Birmingham, AL: Religious Education Press, 1980). For further development, see my "Kerygmatic Theology and Religious Education," in *Theologies of Religious Education*, ed. Randolph Crump Miller (Birmingham, AL: Religious Education Press, 1995), 230–254.

22. See especially Anthony J. Saldarini, *Pharisees, Scribes and Sadducees in Palestinian Society* (Wilmington, DE: Michael Glazier, 1988) and *Matthew's Christian-Jewish Community* (Chicago: University of Chicago Press, 1994); Donald J. Dietrich, *God and Humanity in Auschwitz: Jewish-Christian Relations and Sanctioned Murder* (New Brunswick, NJ: Transaction Publishers, 1995).

23. Mary C. Boys, "Questions Which 'Touch on the Heart of Faith,'" *Religious Education* 76 (November–December 1981): 236–256. Earlier, I had written an essay on the work of Holocaust survivor Elie Wiesel, but I had not yet grappled with implications for religious education. See "Contending with God: The Meaning of Faith in Elie Wiesel," *NICM Journal* (Spring 1978): 75–85.

24. The Sisters of Our Lady of Sion was founded in France in the 1840s for the work of converting Jews, so its present commitment represents a dramatic reversal of the founding vision. I see them as a sort of parable for the church today. See Mary C. Boys, "The Sisters of Sion: From a Conversionist Stance to a Dialogical Way of Life," *Journal of Ecumenical Studies* 31/1–2 (1994): 27–48.

25. See Psalm 122:6.

26. "Religious" educator refers primarily to my concerns with making accessible the knowledge and wisdom of religious traditions, and especially that of Christians. "Theological" educator denotes my interest in the education and formation of professional theologians, clergy, and others who serve in pastoral positions.

27. Over the years, the Christian Scholars Group has had a number of sponsors who pay our travel expenses. When I first joined the group, the Institute for Christian-Jewish Studies in Baltimore was our sponsor. Now the Center for Christian-Jewish Learning at Boston College hosts us.

28. Clark Williamson, *A Guest in the House of Israel: Post-Holocaust Church Theology* (Louisville: John Knox/Westminster, 1993), 9.

29. Among the exceptions, see Gabriel Moran, *Uniqueness: Problems and Paradox in Jewish and Christian Traditions* (Maryknoll, NY: Orbis Books, 1992), and Padraic O'Hare, *The Enduring Covenant: The Education of Christians and the End of Antisemitism* (Valley Forge, PA: Trinity Press International, 1997). Professor Fayette Veverka of Villanova University has also devoted considerable energies to Jewish-Christian relations.

30. The diversity of beliefs and practices under the rubric of "Christianity" is staggering. Linda Woodhead provides a useful heuristic of church Christianity, biblical Christianity, and mystical Christianity. See her *Christianity: A Very Short Introduction* (Oxford: Oxford University Press, 2004).

31. Professor Ingall and I collaborate in teaching a course, "Faith Journeys and the Religious Education of Adults." Students from our respective institutions study contemporary memoirs and autobiographies by Jews and Christians. Although the course does not explicitly revolve around the theological issues in the Jewish-Christian dialogue, we nevertheless engage in profound conversation about matters of faith.

32. Nicholas C. Burbules, *Dialogue in Teaching: Theory and Practice* (New York: Teachers College Press, 1993), 42.

33. See Peter C. Phan, *Being Religious Interreligiously: Asian Perspectives on Interfaith Dialogue* (Maryknoll, NY: Orbis, 2004).

34. Taken from our statement of September 1, 2002, "A Sacred Obligation." See Appendix 2.

35. Mary has taken up this task in *Has God Only One Blessing? Judaism as a Source of Christian Self-Understanding* (New York: Paulist Press, 2000).

36. "Our still open wounds" is taken from the statement of the French bishops, "Declaration of Repentance," in Secretariat for Ecumenical and Interreligious Affairs, National Conference of Catholic Bishops, *Catholics Remember the Holocaust* (Washington, DC: U.S. Catholic Conference, 1998), 32. Historian Jules Isaac coined the phrase "teaching of contempt" to summarize the way Christianity has taught about Jews and Judaism; see his *The Teaching of Contempt: Christian Roots of Anti-Semitism*, trans. Helen Weaver (New York: Holt, Rinehart, and Winston, 1964). This French survivor's audience with Pope John XXIII in 1960 apparently helped to place the church's relations with Jews on the agenda of Vatican II. See the account in Michael Phayer, *The Catholic Church and the Holocaust, 1930–1965* (Bloomington: Indiana University Press, 2000), 203–208.

37. Lewis Weinstein, *The Heretic* (New York: goodnewfiction.com, 2000).

38. "The venomous plant of hatred . . ." is taken from the statement of the French bishops. See n. 36.

39. From the Commission for Religious Relations with the Jews, "We Remember: A Reflection on the Shoah," in *Catholics Remember the Holocaust*, 55.

40. I have written elsewhere in greater detail about my problems with the film and the issues the controversy raises. See my "What We Saw at the Movies," in *Perspectives on* The Passion of the Christ: *Religious Thinkers and Writers Explore the Issues Raised by the Controversial Movie*, ed. Jonathan Burnham (New York: Miramax Books, 2004), 147–163; "Educating for a Faith that Feels *and* Thinks," in *Pondering the Passion: What's at Stake for Christians and Jews?* ed. Philip A. Cunningham (Lanham, MD: Rowman & Littlefield, 2004), 181–192; "I Didn't See Any Antisemitism," *Cross Currents* 54/1 (Spring 2004): 8–15.

41. See Dean P. Béchard, ed., *The Scripture Documents: An Anthology of Official Catholic Teachings* (Collegeville, MN: Liturgical Press, 2001).

42. Peter Steinfels, *A People Adrift: The Crisis of the Roman Catholic Church in America* (New York: Simon and Schuster, 2003), 247.

43. Vanessa Ochs, *Words on Fire: One Woman's Journey into the Sacred* (San Diego: Harcourt Brace Jovanovich, 1990).

44. Schneiders, *Finding the Treasure*, 348. She argues that members of religious communities can embody a vital Catholic Christian spirituality that is able to "provide a stable and secure base for interaction with currents of spirituality that are not explicitly Catholic and, equally importantly, a wisdom context within which to discern what is and what is not compatible with and enriching of Christian faith." She maintains that members of a religious community "can celebrate in the power of age-old Catholic liturgical ritual even as they develop new forms of prayer suitable for this cultural setting" and "can draw on and learn from the wisdom of the Catholic mystical tradition even as they learn from the prayer traditions of other faiths" (349).

CHAPTER 4

Interreligious Teaching and Learning: The Experience

1. In her teaching at Union Theological Seminary, Mary has regularly worked with Christians across the denominational spectrum in dialogue with Jews. Because Christianity is so varied, dialogue becomes even more complicated.

2. *Religious Education* 91/4 (Fall 1996).

3. Mary C. Boys and Sara S. Lee, "The Catholic-Jewish Colloquium: An Experiment in Interreligious Learning," *Religious Education* 91 (Fall 1996): 425.

4. The funding from the Lilly Endowment, $142,375, was granted to the Institute for Christian and Jewish Studies for the Catholic-Jewish Colloquium.

5. Shaye Cohen, *From the Maccabees to the Mishnah* (Philadelphia: Westminster, 1987), and James D. G. Dunn, *The Partings of the Ways* (London: SCM and Trinity Press International, 1991).

6. At the time, Anthony J. Saldarini (d. 2001) was a professor of theology at Boston College and a Catholic scholar of rabbinic Judaism. See Alan J. Avery-Peck, Daniel Harrington, and Jacob Neusner, *When Judaism and Christianity Began: Essays in Memory of Anthony J. Saldarini*, 2 vols., supplements to the *Journal for the Study of Judaism* 85 (Leiden and Boston: Brill, 2004).

7. Edward Flannery, *The Anguish of the Jews*, rev. ed. (New York: Paulist Press, 1985), and Marc Saperstein, *Moments of Crisis in Jewish-Christian Relations* (Philadelphia: Trinity Press International, 1989).

8. Michael A. Signer, a rabbi, holds the Abrams professorship in Jewish Studies at the University of Notre Dame.

9. John A. Coleman, a Jesuit priest and sociologist of religion, was then a professor at the Jesuit School of Theology in Berkeley. Historian Hasia Diner was then teaching at the University of Maryland. When we extended the invitation to Professor Diner, we did not know that she is also the daughter of Holocaust survivors.

10. Celia Deutsch, a New Testament scholar and a Sister of Sion, is a professor at Barnard College in New York City. Elizabeth Losinski is also a Sister of Sion who has worked extensively in Jewish-Christian dialogue in Toronto. Donald Goor is the senior rabbi at Temple Judea in Tarzana, California.

11. Dorothy C. Bass, a historian and ordained minister in the United Church of Christ, is the director of the Valparaiso Project on the Education and Formation of Persons in Faith.

12. Boys and Lee, "The Catholic-Jewish Colloquium," 438.

13. Ibid., 445.

14. Ibid., 444.

15. Although Christians and Jews share all the books of the Jewish Bible (Tanakh), each tradition places the books in a different order. Moreover, the canon of the Catholic Church and the Eastern Orthodox churches includes more books than the canon of Tanakh.

16. Boys and Lee, "The Catholic-Jewish Colloquium," 448.

17. Ibid., 446.

18. Ibid., 449.

19. Neil Gillman is a rabbi and professor at the Jewish Theological Seminary of America in New York City, and John T. Pawlikowski is a priest and professor at Catholic Theological Union in Chicago.

20. Rabbi Deborah Joselow, "The Interdependence of Particularism and Pluralism" (paper delivered to the APRRE Conference, Toronto, Canada, November, 1999).

21. Dr. Fayette B. Veverka, "My Particularism, Your Particularism and Our Pluralism" (paper delivered at the APRRE Conference in Toronto, Canada, November 1999).

22. Unpublished notes from a consultation held March 11–12, 2001.

23. See Appendices 1 and 2.

24. There are two major groups of Lutherans in the United States. The larger is the Evangelical Lutheran Church in America. The Lutheran Church, Missouri Synod, differs from the ELCA in emphasizing the inerrancy of the Bible and is generally more theologically conservative. Another group of Lutherans, the Wisconsin Evangelical Lutheran Synod, broke with the LCMS in 1961.

25. Produced by Auteur Productions, 10010 Newhall Road, Potomac, Maryland 20854; www.jewsandchristians journey.com/the_filmmakers.htm

CHAPTER 5

Toward a Theory of Interreligious Teaching and Learning

1. Donald Finkel, *Teaching with Your Mouth Shut* (Portsmouth, NH: Boynton/Cook, 2000), 137. We have taken the term "collegial teaching" from Finkel.

2. John Merkle, "Bound Together in God," *Religious Education* 91/4 (1996): 551.

3. See Paulo Friere, *Pedagogy of the Oppressed*, trans. Myra Bergman Ramos (New York: Seabury Press, 1970). This is now available in a new translation in *The Paulo Freire Reader*, ed. A. M. A. Freire and Donald Macedo (New York: Continuum, 1998), 67–69. The phrase "receive, retain, and return the words of authorities" is drawn from Mary Field Belenky, Blythe McVicker Clinchy, Nancy Rule Goldberger, and Jill Mattuck Tarule, *Women's Ways of Knowing: The Development of Self, Voice, and Mind* (New York: Basic Books, 1986), 39.

4. Nicholas C. Burbules, *Dialogue in Teaching: Theory and Practice* (New York: Teachers College Press, 1993), 10.

5. Burbules, *Dialogue in Teaching*, 10.

6. Howard Gardner uses the term "interpersonal intelligence" to refer to the ability to interact with others, to understand them, and to be able to interpret their attitudes and behaviors. See

Howard Gardner, *Frames of Mind: The Theory of Multiple Intelligences* (New York: Basic Books, 1983), and Howard Gardner, *Intelligence Reframed: Multiple Intelligences for the 21st Century* (New York: Basic Books, 2000).

7. Dwayne Huebner, "Educational Foundations for Dialogue," *Religious Education* 91/4 (1996): 584.

8. Joseph McDonald, *Teaching: Making Sense of an Uncertain Craft* (New York: Teachers College Press, 1992), 1. The phrase "multiple small uncertainties" is from Maxine Greene, *The Teacher as Stranger* (Belmont, CA: Wadsworth Press, 1973), 220.

9. Stephen Brookfield, *The Skillful Teacher* (San Francisco: Jossey-Bass, 1990), 3.

10. Margret Buchmann, "The Careful Vision: How Practical Is Contemplation in Teaching?" Issue Paper 89–1 (East Lansing: Michigan State University, National Center for Research on Teacher Education, 1989), 16. See also Buchmann and Robert E. Floden, *Detachment and Concern: Conversations in the Philosophy of Teaching and Teacher Education* in *Advances in Contemporary Educational Thought*, vol. 11 (New York: Teachers College Press, 1993).

11. Michael Oakeshott, *Rationalism in Politics and Other Essays* (Indianapolis: Liberty Fund, 1991), 490.

12. Cited in Mary C. Boys and Sara S. Lee, "The Catholic-Jewish Colloquium: An Experiment in Interreligious Learning," *Religious Education* 91/4 (1996): 451.

13. Buchmann, "The Careful Vision," 15.

14. See Donald Schön, *The Reflective Practitioner* (New York: Basic Books, 1983).

15. See Lee S. Shulman, "Knowledge and Teaching: Foundations of the New Reform," *Harvard Educational Review* 57/1 (1987): 1–22. We highly recommend the article from which we prepared this diagram.

16. Typology is a literary technique by which a figure or an event (e.g., the death of Jesus on the cross) is foreshadowed by an earlier figure or event (e.g., the near-death of Isaac on the wood of the altar). The early church writers, following the lead of the New Testament, saw in the story of the sacrifice of Isaac the sacrifice of Jesus on the cross.

17. McDonald, *Teaching*, 1.

18. Stephen Brookfield, *Understanding and Facilitating Adult Learning* (San Francisco: Jossey-Bass, 1986), 139–141.

19. Brookfield, *Understanding and Facilitating Adult Learning*, 135–136. For an extensive analysis of discussion and excellent strategies, see Brookfield and Stephen Preskill, *Discussion as a Way of Teaching: Tools and Techniques for Democratic Classrooms* (San Francisco: Jossey-Bass, 1999).

20. Over the years we have found it useful to consult various typologies of the questioning process. Such typologies provide a sort of map that enables us to consider how wording questions in a certain way will elicit a particular kind of knowledge. See Barbara Gross-Davis, *Tools for Teaching* (San Francisco: Jossey-Bass, 1993), and Norah Morgan and Juliana Saxton, *Teaching Questioning and Learning* (London: Routledge, 1991).

21. Margret Buchmann, "Improving Educating by Talking: Argument or Conversation?" *Teachers College Record* 86/3 (Spring 1985): 441–453; citation, 451.

22. See Jane Vella, *Learning to Listen, Learning to Teach: The Power of Dialogue in Educating Adults,* rev. ed. (San Francisco: Jossey-Bass, 2002).

23. Vella, *Learning to Listen*, 9–10, 71–84.

24. A crucifix is a cross with the image of Jesus on it and is more characteristic of Catholic symbolism than Protestant.

25. Brookfield, *The Skillful Teacher*, 197.

CHAPTER 6

After Auschwitz: Conversations in a Krakow Park

1. "This camp [Auschwitz] has become a symbol of the Holocaust, of genocide and terror, of the violation of basic human rights and of what racism, antisemitism, xenophobia, chauvinism, and intolerance can lead to. The name of the camp has become a sort of cultural code that defines the most negative interpersonal relations. It is a synonym for the breakdown of contemporary civilization and culture." Teresa and Henryk Swiebocki, eds., *Auschwitz: The Residence of Death* (Krakow, Poland: Bialy Kruk), 6.

2. The phrase is from Pope John Paul II, "Message on the Occasion of the Sixtieth Anniversary of the Liberation of the Concentration Camp of Auschwitz-Birkenau," January 27, 2005. See www.bc.edu/research/cjl/meta-elements/texts/documents/johnpaulii/27Jan05_liberation_Auschwitz.htm.

3. There was also Auschwitz III, or Buna at Monowitz, a slave-labor camp to support the I G Farben factory that produced buna (synthetic rubber made from the polymerization of butadiene and sodium). There were eventually twenty-eight sub-camps in the area.

4. See Robert McAfee Brown, *Creative Dislocation: The Movement of Grace* (Nashville: Abingdon, 1980), 18.

5. Dachau, near Munich, was the first concentration camp the Nazis established (1933). Although concentration camps were originally places to house political prisoners, they became slave-labor camps as the war progressed. But some camps were intended primarily for the extermination of Jews: Belzec, Chelmno, Majdanek-Lublin, Sobibor, and Treblinka—all in Poland. Auschwitz-Birkenau was unique insofar as it had a double role: both a slave-labor camp and an extermination camp. "[I]t was easier to do unsavory things in Auschwitz than, for example, in Dachau, which was close to Munich, or in Sachenhausen, near Berlin" (Debórah Dwork and Robert Jan Van Pelt, *Auschwitz* [New York: W. W. Norton, 1996], 282–283). Prisoners suffered terribly in the miserable conditions at all the camps, and many died. But the extermination camps, with their gas chambers and crematoria, enabled the Nazis to annihilate Jews with maximum efficiency.

6. *Yahrzeit* candle: On the anniversary of the death of one's parents, spouse, children, or siblings, Jews are obligated to perform two rituals. The first is the lighting of a 24-hour memorial candle on the Hebrew date of the anniversary. The second is the recitation of the Kaddish (Mourners' Prayer) in the context of a worship service. At Auschwitz, a single *Yahrzeit* candle is lit continuously.

7. Craig S. Smith, "Liberators and Survivors Recall the Auschwitz That Was," *The New York Times* (January 28, 2005); A6.

8. Craig S. Smith, "World Leaders Gather for Auschwitz Ceremony," *The New York Times* (January 27, 2005); A3.

9. See Yaffa Eliach, *There Was Once a World: A 900-Year Chronicle of the Shtetl of Eishyshok* (Boston: Little, Brown, 1998).

10. See Laurence Rees, *Auschwitz: A New History* (New York: Public Affairs, 2005), 42.

11. See Dwork and Van Pelt, *Auschwitz,* 10.

12. According to a February 1943 report submitted to Heinrich Himmler by Oswald Pohl, chief of the SS Main Administration and Economic Office, 824 boxcars of goods were shipped out of Auschwitz, the vast majority sent to the Reich Ministry of Economy. See Dwork and Van Pelt, *Auschwitz,* 323.

13. See Boys and Lee, "The Catholic-Jewish Colloquium," *Religious Education* 91/4 (Fall 1996), also available at www.bc.edu/research/cjl/meta-elements/partners/ERPP/CJC_Contents.htm.

14. Michael Phayer, *The Catholic Church and the Holocaust, 1930–1965* (Bloomington: Indiana University Press, 2000), 122–126.

15. Robert A. Krieg, *Catholic Theologians in Nazi Germany* (New York: Continuum, 2004), 158–159.

16. Ibid., 155.

17. Ibid., 171.

18. See José M. Sánchez, *Pius XII and the Holocaust: Understanding the Controversy* (Washington, DC: Catholic University of America Press, 2002), esp. 172–179.

19. Cited in the German Bishops' Statement of 1995, "Opportunity to Reexamine Relationships with the Jews," in *Catholics Remember the Holocaust* (Washington, DC: Secretariat for Ecumenical and Interreligious Affairs, National Conference of Catholic Bishops, 1998), 11.

20. John Pawlikowski, "The Holocaust: Does It Have Significance for Ethics Today?" (paper delivered at the 33rd Annual Scholars' Conference on the Holocaust and the Churches, Philadelphia, March 2, 2003). www.jcrelations.net/en/?id=1995.

21. Johann-Baptist Metz, *The Emergent Church*, trans. Peter Mann (New York: Crossroad, 1981), 29.

22. Clark Williamson, *A Guest in the House of Israel* (Louisville: Westminster/John Knox, 1993), 9.

23. Jonathan Sacks, "The Holocaust in the Context of Judaism," in *Judaism Transcends Catastrophe: God, Torah, and Israel*

Beyond the Holocaust, vol. 1, ed. Jacob Neusner (Macon, GA: Mercer University Press, 1994), 41.

24. See Deborah Lipstadt, *Denying the Holocaust: The Growing Assault on Truth and Memory* (New York: Plume, 1994). For the story of her confrontation with a Holocaust denier, see her *History on Trial: My Day in Court with David Irving* (New York: Ecco, 2005).

25. Richard Rubinstein, *After Auschwitz: Radical Theology and Contemporary Judaism* (Upper Saddle River, NJ: Prentice-Hall, 1966), quoted in *A Holocaust Reader: Responses to Nazi Extermination,* ed. Michael L. Morgan (Oxford: Oxford University Press, 2001), 94.

26. Michael Rosenak, "Education for Jewish Identification: Theoretical Guidelines," in *Forum on the Jewish People, Zionism, and Israel,* ed. Amnon Hadary (Jerusalem: World Zionist Organization, 1978), 123.

27. See Eliezer Berkovits, *Faith after the Holocaust* (New York: KTAV, 1973); Emil Fackenheim, "Jewish Faith and the Holocaust," in *A Holocaust Reader,* 115–122; Irving Greenberg, "Cloud of Smoke, Pillar of Fire: Judaism, Christianity, and Modernity after the Holocaust," in *Auschwitz: Beginning of a New Era,* ed. Eva Fleischner (New York: KTAV, 1977).

28. Sacks, "The Holocaust in the Context of Judaism," 52.

29. Irving Greenberg, "Judaism, Christianity, and Partnership after the Twentieth Century" in *Christianity in Jewish Terms,* ed. Tikva Frymer-Krensky, David Novak, Peter Ochs, David Fox Sandmel, and Michael Signer (Boulder, CO: Westview Press, 2000), 29.

30. For more information, see www.motl.org.

31. For more information on this project and document, see www.icjs.org/what/njsp/dabruemet.html. The companion statement, "A Sacred Obligation," is available in a number of languages at www.jcrelations.net. See also the book that develops the statement: Mary C. Boys, ed., *Seeing Judaism Anew* (Lanham, MD: Rowman and Littlefield, 2005).

32. See, for example, *Teaching the Holocaust in Catholic Schools: Sixth Holocaust Education Conference* (Greensburg, PA: National Catholic Center for Holocaust Education, Seton Hill University, 2005).

33. Greenberg, "Judaism, Christianity, and Partnership," 28. See also his recent book, *For the Sake of Heaven and Earth: The New Encounter between Judaism and Christianity* (Philadelphia: The Jewish Publication Society, 2004).

34. Irving Greenberg, "Pluralism and Partnership," in *From the Martin Buber House*, vol. 26 (Heppenheim, Germany: Martin Buber House, 1999), 78–81.

35. Greenberg, "Pluralism and Partnership," 72–73.

CHAPTER 7

Jews, Christians and the Land of Israel

1. See Arnold Eisen, *Galut: Modern Jewish Reflections on Homelessness and Homecoming* (Bloomington: Indiana University Press, 1986). Eisen, the Daniel E. Koshland Professor in Jewish Culture and Religion at Stanford University, was named chancellor of the Jewish Theological Seminary of America in April 2006.

2. Barry W. Holtz, *Finding Our Way* (New York: Schocken Books, 1990), 198.

3. *Encyclopaedia Judaica*, vol. 9 (Jerusalem: Keter Publishing House, 1972), 238–251.

4. The Mishnah refers to the entire content of traditional law developed by the end of the second century of the Common Era. The Talmud refers to the comprehensive collections of the discussions by scholars of the Mishnah. There are both Babylonian and Palestinian collections, containing both legal and literary elements. The Midrash is the literary works that contain scriptural interpretations. There are many different collections of Midrash.

5. *Leviticus Rabbah* 13.2, cited in Rabbi Joseph Zahavi, compiler, *Eretz Yisrael in Rabbinic Lore* (Jerusalem: Tehilla Institute, 1962), 60.

6. *Midrash Psalms* 137.6, cited in Reuven Hammer, ed., *The Jerusalem Anthology* (Philadelphia: Jewish Publication Society, 1995), 138.

7. *Yalkut Shimoni Pss.* 836, cited in Hammer, 115.

8. *Encyclopaedia Judaica*, vol. 9 (Jerusalem: Keter Publishing House, 1972), 238–301.

9. www.zionismontheweb.org/zionism_definitions.htm.

10. Theodore Herzl, *The Jewish State,* cited in *The Zionist Idea: A Historical Analysis and Reader,* ed. Arthur Hertzberg (New York: Atheneum, 1969), 204–226.

11. See Arthur Hertzberg, ed., *The Zionist Idea: A Historical Analysis and Reader* and http://www.zionism-israel.com/.

12. For the Declaration of the Establishment of the State of Israel, see www.mfa.gov.il.

13. These numbers do not include Palestinians on the West Bank or Gaza. See Martha Kruger, "Israel: Balancing the Demographics of the Jewish State" (July 2005), www.migrationinformation.org/Profiles/display.cfm?ID=321.

14. For a comprehensive resource on both Zionist history and the modern State of Israel, see Howard M. Sachar, *A History of Israel: From the Rise of Zionism to Our Time* (New York: Alfred A. Knopf, 1996). A more controversial history of the early days of the State of Israel is found in Tom Segev, *1949: The First Israelis* (New York: Henry Holt, 1986).

15. This history is wonderfully recounted in Robert L. Wilken, *The Land Called Holy: Palestine in Christian History and Thought* (New Haven: Yale University Press, 1992).

16. Mary has dealt with this complex relationship in her book, *Has God Only One Blessing? Judaism as a Source of Christian Self-Understanding* (New York: Paulist Press, 2000), esp. 39–74.

17. Reuven Kimmelman, "Rabbi Yohanan and Origen on the Song of Songs: A Third Century Jewish-Christian Disputation," *Harvard Theological Review* 73 (1980): 567–595.

18. For Ezekiel, see: "Thus says the Lord God: This is Jerusalem; I have set her in the center of the nations, with countries all around her" (5:5); "to seize, spoil, and carry off plunder; to assail the waste places that are now inhabited, and the people who were gathered from the nations, who are acquiring cattle and goods, who live at the center of the earth" (38:12). For rabbinic texts, see *M. Kelim* 1:6 (*Mishnah* tractate *Kelim*) and *Midrash Tanhuma, Kedoshim* 10.

19. "Anastasis" is the transliteration of the Greek term for resurrection, and here it refers to the basilica Constantine built to honor the resurrection of Jesus; it was dedicated in 335. For a

succinct account of its complicated history, see Jerome
Murphy-O'Connor, *The Holy Land: An Archaeological Guide
from Earliest Times to 1700*, new ed. (Oxford: Oxford
University Press, 1986), 43–53.

20. Cited in John Wilkinson, *Jerusalem Pilgrims before the Crusades*
(Warminster, England: Aris & Phillips, 1977), 92.

21. Wilken, *The Land Called Holy*, 91.

22. Ibid., 114.

23. Both Jews and Christians, however, suffered from the Fatimid
caliph al-Hākim, who in 1099 ordered the destruction of the
Anastasis and Martyrium of Constantine, legislated that
Christians wear heavy crosses around their necks and Jews a
large block of wood, and desecrated the synagogue in
Jerusalem. This caliph seems to have been demented. See Karen
Armstrong, *Jerusalem: One City, Three Faiths* (New York:
Ballantine Books, 1996), 258–259.

24. Christopher Tyerman defines a crusade as a "war answering
God's command, authorized by a legitimate authority, the pope,
who, by virtue of the power seen as vested in him as Vicar of
Christ, identified the war's object and offered to those who
undertook it full remission of the penalties of confessed sins and
a package of temporal privileges, including church protection of
family and property, immunity from law suits and interest
repayments on debt" (*Fighting for Christendom: Holy War and
the Crusades* [Oxford: Oxford University Press, 2004], 30).

25. Armstrong, *Jerusalem*, 274.

26. Gabriel A. Almond, R. Scott Appleby, and Emmanuel Sivan,
*Strong Religion: The Rise of Fundamentalisms around the
World* (Chicago: The University of Chicago Press, 2003), 3.

27. Armstrong, *Jerusalem*, 294.

28. Marc Saperstein, *Moments of Crisis in Jewish-Christian
Relations* (London: SCM and Philadelphia: Trinity Press
International, 1989), 19.

29. Here I follow the terminology of the Middle East Council of
Churches, which uses "Evangelical" as the rubric for Protestant
churches in that region; this usage should not be confused with
"Evangelical" as understood in North America. For a helpful
introduction, see Betty Jane Bailey and J. Martin Bailey, *Who*

Are the Christians in the Middle East? (Grand Rapids, MI: Wm. B. Eerdmans, 2003). A more scholarly work on the Eastern churches is Ronald Roberson, *The Eastern Christian Churches: A Brief Survey,* 6th ed. (Rome: Edizioni Orientalia Christiana, 1999).

30. Murphy-O'Connor, *The Holy Land,* 43–44.

31. Wilken, *The Land Called Holy,* 254.

32. Charles M. Sennott, *The Body and the Blood: The Holy Land's Christians at the Turn of a New Millennium* (New York: Public Affairs, 2001), 24–25.

33. The ministry of Jesus was centered in the Galilee. In the Gospel of Mark, Jesus teaches from a boat (4:1) and calms a storm on the lake (4:36–41); Mark also makes mention of the crowds that gather around Jesus along the lake (5:21). The Gospel of Matthew depicts the call of the disciples along the Sea of Galilee (4:18–22).

34. For the Sermon on the Mount, see Matthew 5–7. Although there is no firm evidence that Jesus actually preached the sermon there (and Luke's version takes place on a plain [Luke 6:21–49]), the area has been associated with it at least since the fourth-century pilgrim Egeria mentioned it in her letters; see John Wilkinson, *Egeria's Travels* (London: S.P.C.K., 1971). For the multiplication of loaves and fishes, see Mark 6:30–44; the modern church (1982) preserves beautiful mosaics from a mid-fifth-century basilica.

35. For an excellent scholarly anthology on Christian, Roman, and Jewish life in the Galilee, see Lee I. Levine, ed., *The Galilee in Late Antiquity* (New York: Jewish Theological Seminary of America, 1992).

36. Glenn Bowman, "Christian Ideology and the Image of a Holy Land," in *Contesting the Sacred: The Anthropology of Christian Pilgrimage*, ed. John Eade and Michael J. Sallnow (London: Routledge, 1991), 98.

37. Irshad Manji, "How I Learned to Love the Wall," *The New York Times* (March 18, 2006), A15.

38. See David Samuels, "How Arafat Destroyed Palestine," *The Atlantic* 296/2 (September 2005): 60–91.

39. See Ted Conover, "The Checkpoint," *The Atlantic* 297/2 (March 2006): 72–88.

40. Irving Greenberg, "Judaism, Christianity, and Partnership after the Twentieth Century," in *Christianity in Jewish Terms*, ed. Tikva Frymer-Krensky, David Novak, Peter Ochs, David Fox Sandmel, and Michael Signer (Boulder: Westview Press, 2000), 29.

41. John T. Pawlikowski, "Ethical Issues in the Israeli-Palestinian Conflict," in *Beyond Occupation: American, Jewish, Christian, and Palestinian Voices for Peace*, ed. Rosemary Radford Ruether and Marc H. Ellis (Boston: Beacon Press, 1990), 166–169. Pawlikowski argues: "An ethic of solidarity emerging from an affirmation of the continuing centrality of the Shoah for Jewish self-identity must be combined with legitimate aspects of an ethic of survival in any authentic post-Holocaust moral vision" (169).

42. www.sabeel.org/old/reports/easter01.htm. For papers from a Sabeel international conference, see Naim Ateek and Michael Prior, eds., *Holy Land, Hollow Jubilee: God, Justice, and the Palestinians* (London: Melisende, 1999).

43. Hirsh Goodman, "Bring on the Comedians," *The Jerusalem Report* 16/26 (2006): 11.

44. Benny Morris, *Righteous Victims: A History of the Zionist-Arab Conflict, 1881–1999* (New York: Alfred A. Knopf, 1999). Benny Morris is a professor of history at Ben Gurion University in Beer Sheva and noted for his objective treatment of the subject based on significant archival documents. See also www.mideastweb.org/nutshell.htm.

45. Calvin Goldscheider, *Cultures in Conflict: The Arab-Israeli Conflict* (Westport, CT: Greenwood Press, 2001), 15.

APPENDIX 1

In recent years, there has been a dramatic and unprecedented shift in Jewish and Christian relations. Throughout the nearly two millennia of Jewish exile, Christians have tended to characterize Judaism as a failed religion or, at best, a religion that prepared the way for, and is completed in, Christianity. In the decades since the Holocaust, however, Christianity has changed dramatically. An increasing number of official Church bodies, both Roman Catholic and Protestant, have made public statements of their remorse about Christian mistreatment of Jews and Judaism. These statements have declared, furthermore, that Christian teaching and preaching can and must be reformed so that they acknowledge God's enduring covenant with the Jewish people and celebrate the contribution of Judaism to world civilization and to Christian faith itself.

We believe these changes merit a thoughtful Jewish response. Speaking only for ourselves—an interdenominational group of Jewish scholars—we believe it is time for Jews to learn about the efforts of Christians to honor Judaism. We believe it is time for Jews to reflect on what Judaism may now say about Christianity. As a first step, we offer eight brief statements about how Jews and Christians may relate to one another.

Jews and Christians worship the same God. Before the rise of Christianity, Jews were the only worshipers of the God of Israel. But Christians also worship the God of Abraham, Isaac, and Jacob; creator of heaven and earth. While Christian worship is not a viable religious choice for Jews, as Jewish theologians we rejoice that, through Christianity, hundreds of millions of people have entered into relationship with the God of Israel.

Jews and Christians seek authority from the same book—the Bible (what Jews call "Tanakh" and Christians call the "Old Testament"). Turning to it for religious orientation, spiritual enrichment, and communal education, we each take away similar lessons: God created and sustains the universe; God established a covenant with the people Israel, God's revealed word guides Israel to a life of righteousness; and God will ultimately redeem Israel and the whole world. Yet, Jews and Christians interpret the Bible differently on many points. Such differences must always be respected.

Christians can respect the claim of the Jewish people upon the land of Israel. The most important event for Jews since the Holocaust has been the reestablishment of a Jewish state in the Promised Land. As members of a biblically based religion, Christians appreciate that Israel was promised—and given—to

Jews as the physical center of the covenant between them and God. Many Christians support the State of Israel for reasons far more profound than mere politics. As Jews, we applaud this support. We also recognize that Jewish tradition mandates justice for all non-Jews who reside in a Jewish state.

Jews and Christians accept the moral principles of Torah. Central to the moral principles of Torah is the inalienable sanctity and dignity of every human being. All of us were created in the image of God. This shared moral emphasis can be the basis of an improved relationship between our two communities. It can also be the basis of a powerful witness to all humanity for improving the lives of our fellow human beings and for standing against the immoralities and idolatries that harm and degrade us. Such witness is especially needed after the unprecedented horrors of the past century.

Nazism was not a Christian phenomenon. Without the long history of Christian anti-Judaism and Christian violence against Jews, Nazi ideology could not have taken hold nor could it have been carried out. Too many Christians participated in, or were sympathetic to, Nazi atrocities against Jews. Other Christians did not protest sufficiently against these atrocities. But Nazism itself was not an inevitable outcome of Christianity. If the Nazi extermination of the Jews had been fully successful, it would have turned its murderous rage more directly to Christians. We recognize with gratitude those Christians who risked or sacrificed their lives to save Jews during the Nazi regime. With that in mind, we encourage the continuation of recent efforts in Christian theology to repudiate unequivocally contempt of Judaism and the Jewish people. We applaud those Christians who reject this teaching of contempt, and we do not blame them for the sins committed by their ancestors.

The humanly irreconcilable difference between Jews and Christians will not be settled until God redeems the entire world as promised in Scripture. Christians know and serve God through Jesus Christ and the Christian tradition. Jews know and serve God through Torah and the Jewish tradition. That difference will not be settled by one community insisting that it has interpreted Scripture more accurately than the other; nor by exercising political power over the other. Jews can respect Christians' faithfulness to their revelation just as we expect Christians to respect our faithfulness to our revelation. Neither Jew nor Christian should be pressed into affirming the teaching of the other community.

A new relationship between Jews and Christians will not weaken Jewish practice. An improved relationship will not accelerate the cultural and religious assimilation that Jews rightly fear. It will not change traditional Jewish forms of worship, nor increase intermarriage between Jews and non-Jews, nor persuade more Jews to convert to Christianity, nor create a false blending of Judaism and Christianity. We respect Christianity as a faith that originated within Judaism and that still has significant contacts with it. We do not see it as an extension of Judaism. Only if we cherish our own traditions can we pursue this relationship with integrity.

Jews and Christians must work together for justice and peace. Jews and Christians, each in their own way, recognize the unredeemed state of the world as reflected in the persistence of persecution, poverty, and human degradation and misery. Although justice and peace are finally God's, our joint efforts, together with those of other faith communities, will help bring the kingdom of God for which we hope and long. Separately and together, we must work to bring justice and peace to our world. In this enterprise, we are guided by the vision of the prophets of Israel:

> It shall come to pass in the end of days that the mountain of the Lord's house shall be established at the top of the mountains and be exalted above the hills, and the nations shall flow unto it ... and many peoples shall go and say, "Come ye and let us go up to the mountain of the Lord to the house of the God of Jacob and He will teach us of His ways and we will walk in his paths." (Isaiah 2:2–3)

Tikva Frymer-Kensky, University of Chicago
David Novak, University of Toronto
Peter Ochs, University of Virginia
Michael Signer, University of Notre Dame

APPENDIX 2

"A SACRED OBLIGATION:
RETHINKING CHRISTIAN FAITH IN RELATION
TO JUDAISM AND THE JEWISH PEOPLE"

A STATEMENT BY THE CHRISTIAN SCHOLARS
GROUP ON CHRISTIAN-JEWISH RELATIONS

Since its inception in 1969, the Christian Scholars Group has been seeking to develop more adequate Christian theologies of the church's relationship to Judaism and the Jewish people. Pursuing this work for over three decades under varied sponsorship, members of our association of Protestant and Roman Catholic biblical scholars, historians, and theologians have published many volumes on Christian-Jewish relations.

Our work has a historical context. For most of the past two thousand years, Christians have erroneously portrayed Jews as unfaithful, holding them collectively responsible for the death of Jesus and therefore accursed by God. In agreement with many official Christian declarations, we reject this accusation as historically false and theologically invalid. It suggests that God can be unfaithful to the eternal covenant with the Jewish people. We acknowledge with shame the suffering this distorted portrayal has brought upon the Jewish people. We repent of this teaching of contempt. Our repentance requires us to build a new teaching of respect. This task is important at any time, but the deadly crisis in the Middle East and the frightening resurgence of antisemitism worldwide give it particular urgency.

We believe that revising Christian teaching about Judaism and the Jewish people is a central and indispensable obligation of theology in our time. It is essential that Christianity both understand and represent Judaism accurately, not only as a matter of justice for the Jewish people, but also for the integrity of Christian faith, which we cannot proclaim without reference to Judaism. Moreover, since there is a unique bond between Christianity and Judaism, revitalizing our appreciation of Jewish religious life will deepen our Christian faith. We base these convictions on ongoing scholarly research and the official statements of many Christian denominations over the past fifty years.

We are grateful for the willingness of many Jews to engage in dialogue and study with us. We welcomed it when, on September 10, 2000, Jewish scholars sponsored by the Institute of Christian and Jewish Studies in Baltimore issued a historic declaration, *"Dabru Emet*: A Jewish Statement on Christians and Christianity." This document, affirmed by notable rabbis and Jewish scholars, called on Jews to reexamine their understanding of Christianity.

Encouraged by the work of both Jewish and Christian colleagues, we offer the following ten statements for the consideration of our fellow Christians. We urge all Christians to reflect on their faith in light of these statements. For us, this is a sacred obligation.

1. God's covenant with the Jewish people endures forever.

For centuries Christians claimed that their covenant with God replaced or superseded the Jewish covenant. We renounce this claim. We believe that God does not revoke divine promises. We affirm that God is in covenant with both Jews and Christians. Tragically, the entrenched theology of supersessionism continues to influence Christian faith, worship, and practice, even though it has been repudiated by many Christian denominations and many Christians no longer accept it. Our recognition of the abiding validity of Judaism has implications for all aspects of Christian life.

2. Jesus of Nazareth lived and died as a faithful Jew.

Christians worship the God of Israel in and through Jesus Christ. Supersessionism, however, prompted Christians over the centuries to speak of Jesus as an opponent of Judaism. This is historically incorrect. Jewish worship, ethics, and practice shaped Jesus's life and teachings. The scriptures of his people inspired and nurtured him. Christian preaching and teaching today must describe Jesus's earthly life as engaged in the ongoing Jewish quest to live out God's covenant in everyday life.

3. Ancient rivalries must not define Christian-Jewish relations today.

Although today we know Christianity and Judaism as separate religions, what became the church was a movement within the Jewish community for many decades after the ministry and resurrection of Jesus. The destruction of the Jerusalem Temple by Roman armies in the year 70 of the first century caused a crisis among the Jewish people. Various groups, including Christianity and early rabbinic Judaism, competed for leadership in the Jewish community by claiming that they were the true heirs of biblical Israel. The gospels reflect this rivalry in which the disputants exchanged various accusations. Christian charges of hypocrisy and legalism misrepresent Judaism and constitute an unworthy foundation for Christian self-understanding.

4. Judaism is a living faith, enriched by many centuries of development.

Many Christians mistakenly equate Judaism with biblical Israel. However, Judaism, like Christianity, developed new modes of belief and practice in the centuries after the destruction of the Temple. The rabbinic tradition gave new emphasis and understanding to existing practices, such as communal prayer, study of Torah, and deeds of loving-kindness. Thus Jews could live out the covenant in a world without the Temple. Over time they developed an extensive body of interpretive literature that continues to enrich Jewish life, faith, and self-understanding. Christians cannot fully understand Judaism apart from its post-biblical development, which can also enrich and enhance Christian faith.

5. The Bible both connects and separates Jews and Christians.

Some Jews and Christians today, in the process of studying the Bible together, are discovering new ways of reading that provide a deeper appreciation of both traditions. While the two communities draw from the same biblical texts of ancient Israel, they have developed different traditions of interpretation. Christians view these texts through the lens of the New Testament, while Jews understand these scriptures through the traditions of rabbinic commentary.

Referring to the first part of the Christian Bible as the "Old Testament" can wrongly suggest that these texts are obsolete. Alternative expressions—"Hebrew Bible," "First Testament," or "Shared Testament"—although also problematic, may better express the church's renewed appreciation of the ongoing power of these scriptures for both Jews and Christians.

6. Affirming God's enduring covenant with the Jewish people has consequences for Christian understandings of salvation.

Christians meet God's saving power in the person of Jesus Christ and believe that this power is available to all people in him. Christians have therefore taught for centuries that salvation is available only through Jesus Christ. With their recent realization that God's covenant with the Jewish people is eternal, Christians can now recognize in the Jewish tradition the redemptive power of God at work. If Jews, who do not share our faith in Christ, are in a saving covenant with God, then Christians need new ways of understanding the universal significance of Christ.

7. Christians should not target Jews for conversion.

In view of our conviction that Jews are in an eternal covenant with God, we renounce missionary efforts directed at converting Jews. At the same time, we welcome opportunities for Jews and Christians to bear witness to their respective experiences of God's saving ways. Neither can properly claim to possess knowledge of God entirely or exclusively.

8. Christian worship that teaches contempt for Judaism dishonors God.

The New Testament contains passages that have frequently generated negative attitudes toward Jews and Judaism. The use of these texts in the context of worship increases the likelihood of hostility toward Jews. Christian anti-Jewish theology has also shaped worship in ways that denigrate Judaism and foster contempt for Jews. We urge church leaders to examine scripture readings, prayers, the structure of the lectionaries, preaching and hymns to remove distorted images of Judaism. A reformed Christian liturgical life would express a new relationship with Jews and thus honor God.

9. We affirm the importance of the land of Israel for the life of the Jewish people.

The land of Israel has always been of central significance to the Jewish people. However, Christian theology charged that the Jews had condemned themselves to homelessness by rejecting God's Messiah. Such supersessionism precluded any possibility for Christian understanding of Jewish attachment to the land of Israel. Christian theologians can no longer avoid this crucial issue, especially in light of the complex and persistent conflict over the land. Recognizing that both Israelis and Palestinians have the right to live in peace and security in a homeland of their own, we call for efforts that contribute to a just peace among all the peoples in the region.

10. Christians should work with Jews for the healing of the world.

For almost a century, Jews and Christians in the United States have worked together on important social issues, such as the rights of workers and civil rights. As violence and terrorism intensify in our time, we must strengthen our common efforts in the work of justice and peace to which both the prophets of Israel and Jesus summon us. These common efforts by Jews and Christians offer a vision of human solidarity and provide models of collaboration with people of other faith traditions.

Signed by members of the

CHRISTIAN SCHOLARS GROUP ON
CHRISTIAN-JEWISH RELATIONS

Institutions are listed only for identification purposes.

Dr. Norman Beck
Poehlmann Professor of
Biblical Theology and
Classical Languages
Texas Lutheran University
Seguin, Texas

Dr. Mary C. Boys, SNJM
Skinner & McAlpin
Professor of Practical
Theology
Union Theological Seminary
New York City, New York

Dr. Rosann Catalano
Roman Catholic Staff
Scholar
Institute for Christian &
Jewish Studies
Baltimore, Maryland

Dr. Philip A. Cunningham
Executive Director
Center for Christian-
Jewish Learning
Boston College
Chestnut Hill, Massachusetts

Dr. Celia Deutsch, NDS
Adj. Assoc. Prof. of Religion
Barnard College/Columbia
University
New York City, New York

Dr. Alice L. Eckardt
Professor emerita of
Religion Studies
Lehigh University
Bethlehem, Pennsylvania

Dr. Eugene J. Fisher
U.S. Conference of Catholic
Bishops' Committee
for Ecumenical and
Interreligious Affairs
Washington, D.C.

Dr. Eva Fleischner
Montclair (NJ) State
University, emerita
Claremont, California

Dr. Deirdre Good
General Theological Seminary
of the Episcopal Church
New York City, New York

Dr. Walter Harrelson
Distinguished Professor emer-
itus of Hebrew Bible
Vanderbilt University
Nashville, Tennessee

Rev. Michael McGarry, CSP
Tantur Ecumenical Institute
Jerusalem

Dr. John C. Merkle
Professor of Theology
College of St. Benedict
St. Joseph, Minnesota

Dr. John T. Pawlikowski, OSM
Professor of Social Ethics
Director, Catholic-Jewish
Studies Program
Catholic Theological Union
Chicago, Illinois

Dr. Peter A. Pettit
Institute for Christian-Jewish
Understanding
Muhlenberg College
Allentown, Pennsylvania

Dr. Peter C. Phan
The Warren-Blanding Prof-
essor of Religion and Culture
The Catholic University of
America Washington, D.C.

Dr. Jean Pierre Ruiz
Associate Professor and
Chair
Dept. of Theology and
Religious Studies
St. John's University,
New York City, New York

Dr. Franklin Sherman
Associate for Interfaith
Relations
Evangelical Lutheran Church
in America
Allentown, Pennsylvania

Dr. Joann Spillman
Professor and Chair
Dept. of Theology and
Religious Studies
Rockhurst University
Kansas City, Missouri

Dr. John T. Townsend
Visiting Lecturer on Jewish
Studies
Harvard Divinity School
Cambridge, Massachusetts

Dr. Joseph Tyson
Professor emeritus of
Religious Studies
Southern Methodist
University
Dallas, Texas

Dr. Clark M. Williamson
Indiana Professor of
Christian Thought, emeritus
Christian Theological
Seminary
Indianapolis, Indiana

SUGGESTIONS FOR FURTHER READING

Armstrong, Karen. *Jerusalem: One City, Three Faiths*. New York: Ballantine, 1997.

Barnett, Victoria J. *Bystanders: Conscience and Complicity During the Holocaust*. Westport, CT, and London: Praeger, 2000.

Berling, Judith. *Understanding Other Religious Worlds: A Guide for Interreligious Education*. Maryknoll, NY: Orbis, 2004.

Borowsky Irvin, ed. *Rebuilding the Broken Bridges between Christians and Jews*. New York: Crossroad, 2004.

Boys, Mary C. *Has God Only One Blessing? Judaism as a Source of Christian Self-Understanding*. New York and Mahwah, NJ: Paulist Press, 2000.

———, ed. *Seeing Judaism Anew: Christianity's Sacred Obligation*. Lanham, MD: Rowman and Littlefield, 2005.

Brookfield, Stephen. *The Skillful Teacher*. San Francisco: Jossey-Bass, 1990.

Brookfield, Stephen, and Stephen Preskill. *Discussion as a Way of Teaching*. 2nd ed. San Francisco: Jossey-Bass, 2005.

Burbules, Nicholas C. *Dialogue in Teaching: Theory and Practice*. New York: Teachers College Press, 1993.

Cohen, Steven M., and Arnold M. Eisen. *The Jew Within: Self, Family, and Community in America*. Bloomington and Indianapolis: Indiana University Press, 2000.

Eck, Diana. *Encountering God: A Spiritual Journey from Bozeman to Banaras*. Boston: Beacon Press, 1993.

Eisen, Arnold. *Galut: Modern Jewish Reflections on Homelessness and Homecoming*. Bloomington: Indiana University Press, 1986.

Gillman, Rabbi Neil. *The Jewish Approach to God: A Brief Introduction for Christians*. Woodstock, VT: Jewish Lights Publishing, 2003.

Greenberg, Irving. *For the Sake of Heaven and Earth: The New Encounter between Judaism and Christianity*. Philadelphia: Jewish Publication Society, 2004.

Hertzberg, Arthur, ed. *The Zionist Idea: A Historical Analysis and Reader*. New York: Athenaeum, 1969.

Hoffman, Lawrence A., ed. *The Land of Israel: Jewish Perspectives*. Notre Dame, IN: University of Notre Dame Press, 1986.

Holtz, Barry W. *Finding Our Way*. New York: Schocken Books, 1990.

Kenny, Anthony. *Catholics, Jews, and the State of Israel*. New York and Mahwah, NJ: Paulist Press, 1993.

Kessler, Edward, and Neil Wenborn, eds. *A Dictionary of Jewish-Christian Relations*. Cambridge: Cambridge University Press and Cambridge Centre for the Study of Jewish-Christian Relations, 2005.

Korn, Eugene B., and John T. Pawlikowski, eds. *Two Faiths, One Covenant? Jewish and Christian Identity in the Presence of the Other*. Lanham, MD: Rowman and Littlefield, 2005.

Krieg, Robert A. *Catholic Theologians in Nazi Germany.* New York: Continuum, 2004.

Merkle, John C. ed., *Faith Transformed: Christian Encounters with Jews and Judaism.* Collegeville, MN: Liturgical Press, 2003.

Morris, Benny. *Righteous Victims: A History of the Zionist-Arab Conflict, 1881–1999.* New York: Alfred A. Knopf, 1999.

Sacks, Rabbi Jonathan. *To Heal a Fractured World: The Ethics of Responsibility.* New York: Schocken, 2005.

Sánchez, José. *Pius XII and the Holocaust: Understanding the Controversy.* Washington, DC: Catholic University of America Press, 2002.

Sandmel, David, Rosann M. Catalano, and Christopher M. Leighton. *Irreconcilable Differences? A Learning Resource for Jews and Christians.* Boulder: Westview Press, 2001.

Sennott, Charles M. *The Body and the Blood: The Holy Land's Christians at the Turn of a New Millennium.* New York: Public Affairs, 2001.

Shulman, Lee S. "Knowledge and Teaching: Foundations of the New Reform," *Harvard Educational Review* 57/1 (1987): 1–22

Talvacchia, Kathleen T. *Critical Minds and Discerning Hearts: A Spirituality of Multicultural Teaching.* St. Louis: Chalice Press, 2003.

Vella, Jane. *Learning to Listen, Learning to Teach: The Power of Dialogue in Educating Adults.* rev. ed. San Francisco: Jossey-Bass, 2002.

Wilken, Robert L. *The Land Called Holy: Palestine in Christian History and Thought.* New Haven and London: Yale University Press, 1992.

INDEX

Judaism / Christianity

Christians and Jews in Dialogue: Learning in the Presence of the Other
by Mary C. Boys and Sara S. Lee; Foreword by Dorothy C. Bass
Inspires renewed commitment to dialogue between religious traditions and illuminates how it should happen. Explains the transformative work of creating environments for Jews and Christians to study together and enter the dynamism of the other's religious tradition.
6 x 9, 256 pp, HC, 978-1-59473-144-0 **$21.99**

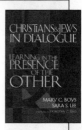

Healing the Jewish-Christian Rift
Growing Beyond Our Wounded History
by Ron Miller and Laura Bernstein; Foreword by Dr. Beatrice Bruteau
Traces the Jewish-Christian schism to its very source in the first book of the New Testament, the Gospel of Matthew, and takes a renewed look at Matthew.
6 x 9, 288 pp, Quality PB, 978-1-59473-139-6 **$18.99**

Introducing My Faith and My Community: The Jewish Outreach Institute Guide for the Christian in a Jewish Interfaith Relationship
by Rabbi Kerry M. Olitzky
Seeks to introduce readers to Judaism and Jewish life in easy-to-understand terms and language.
6 x 9, 176 pp, Quality PB, 978-1-58023-192-3 **$16.99** *(a Jewish Lights book)*

The Jewish Approach to God: A Brief Introduction for Christians
by Rabbi Neil Gillman 5½ x 8½, 192 pp, Quality PB, 978-1-58023-190-9 **$16.95** *(a Jewish Lights book)*

Jewish Holidays: A Brief Introduction for Christians
by Rabbi Kerry M. Olitzky and Rabbi Daniel Judson
5½ x 8½, 176 pp, Quality PB, 978-1-58023-302-6 **$16.99** *(a Jewish Lights book)*

Jewish Ritual: A Brief Introduction for Christians
by Rabbi Kerry M. Olitzky and Rabbi Daniel Judson
5½ x 8½, 144 pp, Quality PB, 978-1-58023-210-4 **$14.99** *(a Jewish Lights book)*

Jewish Spirituality: A Brief Introduction for Christians
by Rabbi Lawrence Kushner
5½ x 8½, 112 pp, Quality PB, 978-1-58023-150-3 **$12.95** *(a Jewish Lights book)*

A Jewish Understanding of the New Testament
by Rabbi Samuel Sandmel; new Preface by Rabbi David Sandmel
Without compromising his Jewish identity or encouraging any traditional Jewish stereotypes about the New Testament, Rabbi Sandmel offers an enlightened view of Christian beliefs and encourages readers to acknowledge their common humanity with people of all religions.
5½ x 8½, 368 pp, Quality PB, 978-1-59473-048-1 **$19.99**

We Jews and Jesus
Exploring Theological Differences for Mutual Understanding
by Rabbi Samuel Sandmel; new Preface by Rabbi David Sandmel A Classic Reprint
Written in a non-technical way for the layperson, this candid and forthright look at the what and why of the Jewish attitude toward Jesus is a clear and forceful exposition that guides both Christians and Jews in relevant discussion.
6 x 9, 192 pp, Quality PB, 978-1-59473-208-9 **$16.99**

Or phone, fax, mail or e-mail to: SKYLIGHT PATHS Publishing
Sunset Farm Offices, Route 4 • P.O. Box 237 • Woodstock, Vermont 05091
Tel: (802) 457-4000 • Fax: (802) 457-4004 • www.skylightpaths.com
Credit card orders: (800) 962-4544 (8:30AM–5:30PM ET Monday–Friday)
Generous discounts on quantity orders. SATISFACTION GUARANTEED. Prices subject to change.

Midrash Fiction / Folktales

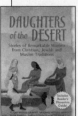

Abraham's Bind & Other Bible Tales of Trickery, Folly, Mercy and Love by Michael J. Caduto
New retellings of episodes in the lives of familiar biblical characters explore relevant life lessons.
6 x 9, 224 pp, HC, 978-1-59473-186-0 **$19.99**

Daughters of the Desert: Stories of Remarkable Women from Christian, Jewish and Muslim Traditions by Claire Rudolf Murphy, Meghan Nuttall Sayres, Mary Cronk Farrell, Sarah Conover and Betsy Wharton
Breathes new life into the old tales of our female ancestors in faith. Uses traditional scriptural passages as starting points, then with vivid detail fills in historical context and place. Chapters reveal the voices of Sarah, Hagar, Huldah, Esther, Salome, Mary Magdalene, Lydia, Khadija, Fatima and many more. Historical fiction ideal for readers of all ages. Quality paperback includes reader's discussion guide.
5½ x 8½, 192 pp, Quality PB, 978-1-59473-106-8 **$14.99**
HC, 192 pp, 978-1-893361-72-0 **$19.95**

The Triumph of Eve & Other Subversive Bible Tales
by Matt Biers-Ariel
Many people were taught and remember only a one-dimensional Bible. These engaging retellings are the antidote to this—they're witty, often hilarious, always profound, and invite you to grapple with questions and issues that are often hidden in the original text.
5½ x 8½, 192 pp, HC, 978-1-59473-040-5 **$19.99**

Also avail.: **The Triumph of Eve Teacher's Guide**
8½ x 11, 44 pp, PB, 978-1-59473-152-5 **$8.99**

Wisdom in the Telling
Finding Inspiration and Grace in Traditional Folktales and Myths Retold
by Lorraine Hartin-Gelardi
6 x 9, 224 pp, HC, 978-1-59473-185-3 **$19.99**

Religious Etiquette / Reference

How to Be a Perfect Stranger, 4th Edition: The Essential Religious Etiquette Handbook Edited by Stuart M. Matlins and Arthur J. Magida
The indispensable guidebook to help the well-meaning guest when visiting other people's religious ceremonies. A straightforward guide to the rituals and celebrations of the major religions and denominations in the United States and Canada from the perspective of an interested guest of any other faith, based on information obtained from authorities of each religion. Belongs in every living room, library and office. Covers:
African American Methodist Churches • Assemblies of God • Bahá'í • Baptist • Buddhist • Christian Church (Disciples of Christ) • Christian Science (Church of Christ, Scientist) • Churches of Christ • Episcopalian and Anglican • Hindu • Islam • Jehovah's Witnesses • Jewish • Lutheran • Mennonite/Amish • Methodist • Mormon (Church of Jesus Christ of Latter-day Saints) • Native American/First Nations • Orthodox Churches • Pentecostal Church of God • Presbyterian • Quaker (Religious Society of Friends) • Reformed Church in America/Canada • Roman Catholic • Seventh-day Adventist • Sikh • Unitarian Universalist • United Church of Canada • United Church of Christ
6 x 9, 432 pp, Quality PB, 978-1-59473-140-2 **$19.99**

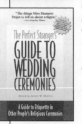

The Perfect Stranger's Guide to Funerals and Grieving Practices: A Guide to Etiquette in Other People's Religious Ceremonies Edited by Stuart M. Matlins
6 x 9, 240 pp, Quality PB, 978-1-893361-20-1 **$16.95**

The Perfect Stranger's Guide to Wedding Ceremonies: A Guide to Etiquette in Other People's Religious Ceremonies Edited by Stuart M. Matlins
6 x 9, 208 pp, Quality PB, 978-1-893361-19-5 **$16.95**

Spirituality & Crafts

The Knitting Way: A Guide to Spiritual Self-Discovery
by Linda Skolnik and Janice MacDaniels
7 x 9, 240 pp, Quality PB, 978-1-59473-079-5 **$16.99**

The Quilting Path
A Guide to Spiritual Discovery through Fabric, Thread and Kabbalah
by Louise Silk
7 x 9, 192 pp, Quality PB, 978-1-59473-206-5 **$16.99**

Spiritual Practice

Divining the Body
Reclaim the Holiness of Your Physical Self *by Jan Phillips*
A practical and inspiring guidebook for connecting the body and soul in spiritual practice. Leads you into a milieu of reverence, mystery and delight, helping you discover your body as a pathway to the Divine.
8 x 8, 256 pp, Quality PB, 978-1-59473-080-1 **$16.99**

Finding Time for the Timeless: Spirituality in the Workweek
by John McQuiston II
Simple, refreshing stories that provide you with examples of how you can refocus and enrich your daily life using prayer or meditation, ritual and other forms of spiritual practice. 5½ x 6¾, 208 pp, HC, 978-1-59473-035-1 **$17.99**

The Gospel of Thomas
A Guidebook for Spiritual Practice *by Ron Miller; Translations by Stevan Davies*
An innovative guide to bring a new spiritual classic into daily life.
6 x 9, 160 pp, Quality PB, 978-1-59473-047-4 **$14.99**

Earth, Water, Fire, and Air: Essential Ways of Connecting to Spirit
by Cait Johnson 6 x 9, 224 pp, HC, 978-1-893361-65-2 **$19.95**

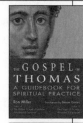

Labyrinths from the Outside In: Walking to Spiritual Insight—A Beginner's Guide
by Donna Schaper and Carole Ann Camp
6 x 9, 208 pp, b/w illus. and photos, Quality PB, 978-1-893361-18-8 **$16.95**

Practicing the Sacred Art of Listening: A Guide to Enrich Your Relationships
and Kindle Your Spiritual Life—The Listening Center Workshop
by Kay Lindahl 8 x 8, 176 pp, Quality PB, 978-1-893361-85-0 **$16.95**

Releasing the Creative Spirit: Unleash the Creativity in Your Life
by Dan Wakefield 7 x 10, 256 pp, Quality PB, 978-1-893361-36-2 **$16.95**

The Sacred Art of Bowing: Preparing to Practice
by Andi Young 5½ x 8½, 128 pp, b/w illus., Quality PB, 978-1-893361-82-9 **$14.95**

The Sacred Art of Chant: Preparing to Practice
by Ana Hernández 5½ x 8½, 192 pp, Quality PB, 978-1-59473-036-8 **$15.99**

The Sacred Art of Fasting: Preparing to Practice
by Thomas Ryan, CSP 5½ x 8½, 192 pp, Quality PB, 978-1-59473-078-8 **$15.99**

The Sacred Art of Forgiveness: Forgiving Ourselves and Others through God's Grace
by Marcia Ford 8 x 8, 176 pp, Quality PB, 978-1-59473-175-4 **$16.99**

The Sacred Art of Listening: Forty Reflections for Cultivating a Spiritual Practice
by Kay Lindahl; Illustrations by Amy Schnapper
8 x 8, 160 pp, b/w illus., Quality PB, 978-1-893361-44-7 **$16.99**

The Sacred Art of Lovingkindness: Preparing to Practice
by Rabbi Rami Shapiro; Foreword by Marcia Ford
5½ x 8½, 176 pp, Quality PB, 978-1-59473-151-8 **$16.99**

Sacred Speech: A Practical Guide for Keeping Spirit in Your Speech
by Rev. Donna Schaper 6 x 9, 176 pp, Quality PB, 978-1-59473-068-9 **$15.99**
HC, 978-1-893361-74-4 **$21.95**

About SKYLIGHT PATHS Publishing

SkyLight Paths Publishing is creating a place where people of different spiritual traditions come together for challenge and inspiration, a place where we can help each other understand the mystery that lies at the heart of our existence.

Through spirituality, our religious beliefs are increasingly becoming a part of our lives—rather than *apart* from our lives. While many of us may be more interested than ever in spiritual growth, we may be less firmly planted in traditional religion. Yet, we do want to deepen our relationship to the sacred, to learn from our own as well as from other faith traditions, and to practice in new ways.

SkyLight Paths sees both believers and seekers as a community that increasingly transcends traditional boundaries of religion and denomination—people wanting to learn from each other, *walking together, finding the way.*

For your information and convenience, at the back of this book we have provided a list of other SkyLight Paths books you might find interesting and useful. They cover the following subjects:

Buddhism / Zen	Gnosticism	Mysticism
Catholicism	Hinduism /	Poetry
Children's Books	Vedanta	Prayer
Christianity	Inspiration	Religious Etiquette
Comparative	Islam / Sufism	Retirement
Religion	Judaism / Kabbalah /	Spiritual Biography
Current Events	Enneagram	Spiritual Direction
Earth-Based	Meditation	Spirituality
Spirituality	Midrash Fiction	Women's Interest
Global Spiritual	Monasticism	Worship
Perspectives		

Or phone, fax, mail or e-mail to: SKYLIGHT PATHS Publishing
Sunset Farm Offices, Route 4 • P.O. Box 237 • Woodstock, Vermont 05091
Tel: (802) 457-4000 • Fax: (802) 457-4004 • www.skylightpaths.com
Credit card orders: (800) 962-4544 (8:30AM–5:30PM ET Monday–Friday)
Generous discounts on quantity orders. SATISFACTION GUARANTEED. Prices subject to change.